D1486127

Highdays and Holidays

by the same author

GRAN'S DRAGON

Highdays and Holidays

MARGARET JOY

illustrated by Juliet Renny

FABER AND FABER
London · Boston

First published in 1981
by Faber and Faber Limited
3 Queen Square London WC1N 3AU
Printed in Great Britain by
Redwood Burn Ltd, Trowbridge, Wiltshire
All rights reserved

Text © Margaret Joy, 1981
Illustrations © Faber and Faber Limited, 1981

British Library Cataloguing in Publication Data

Joy, Margaret
Highdays and holidays.
1. Religious calendars – Juvenile literature
I. Title
291.3'6   BL590

ISBN 0–571–11771–6

Contents

Illustrations

Acknowledgements

The lines on page 93 are taken from "In Flanders' Fields" by John McCrae, first published in *Punch* in 1915.

The passage from *The Country Child* by Alison Uttley on page 110 is reprinted by permission of Faber and Faber Ltd.

The author is grateful to Rabbi Andrew Goldstein, Professor S. N. Bharadwaj, and Mr. Arthur Giles and Mr. Maurice Lynch of the West London Institute of Higher Education (Religious Education In-Service Training and Resources Centre) for advice and information on Jewish, Hindu, Buddhist and Muslim festivals.

Foreword

The life of each of us is full of "highdays": exciting days which we look forward to – like school trips, birthdays, visits to the circus or the theatre – and which we love to remember afterwards.

The highdays mentioned in this book are days which many people can share – whole families, whole villages, sometimes whole nations – like Bonfire Night, Pancake Day, or Independence Day in the United States of America. They are days on which people have been having a 'high old time' for many years, sometimes for centuries.

Holidays used to be 'holy days' in the calendar, when there was a rest from everyday work and people celebrated in honour of a particular saint or happening in the Church's year: like St. George's Day, Whitsun or Christmas.

Holy days were often printed in red in the calendar to remind people that they were special days, so they came to be known as "red letter days". Some of these holy days are many centuries old too, and all countries and races of people have their own.

In this book you can read a little about some of the best known highdays and holy days. There are many more in other parts of the world, and you will probably know of some festivities not mentioned here.

Highdays and holidays are very important, because they bring something special into everyday life; take part in them and enjoy them as much as you can.

MARGARET JOY

New Year's Eve and New Year's Day
31st December and 1st January

31st December is the last day of the year. It is still part of the Christmas season, and is often celebrated by parties which go on past midnight, so that a toast can be drunk to the New Year, directly the clock shows that 1st January has begun.

The Romans chose to name the first month of the year after Janus, the god who looked after beginnings and doors and entrances. Since he was supposed to have a face at the front and at the back, he was able to look backwards and forwards at the same time – very useful for a doorkeeper. So at midnight on 31st December the Romans imagined him looking back at the Old Year and forward to the New.

All over the Western world people still do that. In London crowds gather in Trafalgar Square or on the steps of St. Paul's Cathedral. As the clocks strike midnight there is a moment or two of silence, then cheering breaks out and everyone starts to cross arms and link hands to sing "Auld Lang Syne". This song was written by Robert Burns only about two hundred years ago, but it has become closely associated with New Year, or Hogmanay, as the spirited celebrations are called in Scotland.

The tradition of Hogmanay is connected with the old winter festivities enjoyed by the Norsemen centuries ago. These were concerned with fire or light, and were meant to encourage the sun to return. On New Year's Eve at Stonehaven in Kincardineshire fishermen still fill balls of wire netting with ropes and rags soaked in paraffin. These balls are set alight and young men carry them through the town, swinging them above their heads as they go. Similarly, in Allendale, Northumberland, young men of the

15

village parade through the streets with wooden tubs of burning tar on their heads.

Both in the North of England and in Scotland, "first footing" is considered very important. The first person to enter the house when New Year has begun must be a man, never a woman, and he must be dark-haired, never fair or red-haired or with eyebrows which meet in the middle! Ideally he should be carrying a piece of coal, bread, and money or salt; these ensure that the household will enjoy warmth, food and wealth in the coming year.

In more southerly parts of Britain, Morris dances are often performed on Boxing Day and New Year's Day. One dance is carried out with swords, and at the finale one man's head is "cut off" (symbolizing the end of the Old Year) and instantly restored (symbolizing the beginning of the New Year).

Many people make "good resolutions" on 1st January, resolving to behave better or more sensibly during the coming year. One of these good resolutions is often to keep a diary, starting on New Year's Day.

The noisiest celebrations on 1st January must be in Italy, where, on the stroke of midnight, old furniture, broken crockery, torn books, pillows and broken kitchen appliances come hurtling down from windows to land on the street below with a vibrating crash! Italians save some of their junk for this very moment and enjoy throwing the troubles of the Old Year out of the window. In this way they face the New Year much more cheerfully.

16

The Chinese New Year:
Mid-January – mid-February

Not everyone thinks of the New Year as beginning with January. The Chinese calendar is different from ours and is based on the phases of the moon, so the date of their New Year varies. It is held on the day of the second new moon after 22nd December, so it falls between mid-January and mid-February.

The Chinese call the twelve signs of the zodiac after the only twelve animals who, according to the legend, answered the summons of the Buddha. They were the monkey, the cockerel, the sheep, the dog, the pig, the rat, the ox, the tiger, the hare, the dragon, the snake and the horse. Each year has its particular sign. 1980 was the year of the monkey, 1981 the year of the cockerel, and so on.

Many people of Chinese origin have found work in restaurants and shops in Soho, London, as well as in other cities of Britain. They try to celebrate their New Year with just as much noise and gaiety as their families did in China. Celebrations begin on their

A Chinese dragon

17

New Year's Eve, when a "dragon" (which looks rather like a lion) leads a procession through the streets of Soho. The master of each house opens the front door (to fortune) in much the same way as Scots open the door to welcome a "first footer". At midnight firecrackers, rather like jumping-jacks, are let off and continue to go off throughout the festival, which usually lasts about three days.

Streets, houses and temples are decorated with flags and lanterns of all shapes and colours. Peach and plum blossom, daffodils and chrysanthemums are favourite decorations, as well as models of fish, which are often coloured gold to symbolize wealth. Incense is burnt and pictures of gods are painted and stuck on doors to protect homes from evil spirits. Children love all these colourful festivities and hope to find the outline of a dragon by their bed formed in coins; this brings them good luck. They may also receive lucky money in red envelopes.

This is a holiday time, when members of families get together to exchange presents and enjoy festive meals. Pork is the traditional meat and favourite dishes are steamed rice balls, lychees, longans, lotus seeds and red dates.

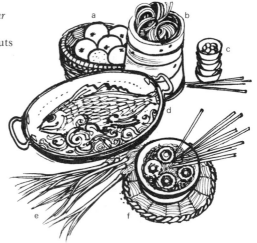

Party food for the Chinese New Year
a oranges   b starch noodles
c radishes   d fish with bean sprouts
e spring onions (scallions)
f fried rice with mushrooms

18

New Year is also a time to do all those jobs which have been waiting to be done: getting your hair cut, paying off your debts, making up family tiffs and cleaning your house. Families also remember those members who have died; they pray to their ancestors and ask for blessings for the living in the year to come.

So the Chinese celebrate with fun and rejoicing, but they also keep the New Year as a religious festival which links the living with their dead ancestors.

Rosh Hashanah, the Jewish New Year
late September – early October

In Biblical times the Hebrews celebrated their New Year in the autumn – at the end of all their work in the fields. The old year had ended, the new year had begun.

That is why Jews, descendants of the Hebrews, celebrate their New Year in autumn, in September or early October. The date in the English calendar varies from year to year, since the Jewish calendar is based on the moon and the English on the sun. The Hebrews began each new month at a new moon and so there will always be a new moon at Rosh Hashanah.

Like all Jewish festivals, the New Year or Rosh Hashanah actually begins at sunset – the day lasting until the next sunset. As it gets dark, the holy day and New Year are welcomed in the Jewish home. First, two candles are lit, usually by the mother. Then the father takes a cup of wine, all the family say a blessing over the wine, and then all drink it. Then they say the blessing over a special loaf of bread called a challah. The family follows this ritual every Sabbath eve –

19

but usually the challah is in the form of a plaited loaf with poppy seeds on top. For Rosh Hashanah a round loaf is used, to show that the seasons go round and New Year is here.

Next comes the sticky part – all the family take pieces of apple, dip them in honey and say, "May the New Year be for us a good and sweet year". Then all eat the apple – followed by loud licking of fingers!

Some will go to Synagogue on New Year's Eve, but most will go the following morning. The rabbi and cantor (who leads the singing) wear white robes.

The Torah is the parchment scroll containing the first five books of the Bible. Jews read from it every Sabbath and holy day. The story on Rosh Hashanah tells of God commanding Abraham to take his son, Isaac, and go to a distant mountain to offer him as a sacrifice. In the end Abraham is prevented from killing his son, and instead sacrifices a ram he finds nearby, caught by its long horns in a bush. Some say the story teaches us that God wants us to serve him through life, not death.

A Moroccan Jew blowing the shofar

We remember the poor ram – for in every Synagogue a Ram's Horn or Shofar is blown many times on Rosh Hashanah. It not only recalls the story of Abraham and Isaac, but reminds the Jews that it is time to repent of their sins. Ten days after Rosh Hashanah will come Yom Kippur – the Day of Atonement –

20

when Jews fast all day, spending most of it in Synagogue and asking God to forgive them for their sins in the past year. Only when they have repented are they ready for a real new year.

After Synagogue on Rosh Hashanah all go home for a festive lunch. The room will be decorated with the New Year cards sent by family and friends. The cards give the same greeting as the family used when meeting their friends after the Synagogue service: "L'shanah Tovah" – "Have a good New Year".

Diwali, the Hindu New Year
End of October – beginning of November

Diwali is the Indian New Year, the "Festival of Lights". Various stories are told about Diwali in different parts of India, but the best known is this Hindu event: a prince, Rama, rescued his wife, Sita, from the ten-headed, ten-armed demon king, Ravana.

Ravana, the demon king

When they returned in triumph for their coronation they were guided back to their country by thousands of clay lamps (diva or deepa) which the rejoicing people had set out for them.

21

(Sikhs also celebrate the festival as a reminder of the time when their sixth Guru or spiritual teacher, Hargobind, was released from prison.)

Before the five-day celebrations start, Hindus clean their homes thoroughly, just as the people of the royal city of Ayodhaya cleaned and polished their homes to welcome Rama and Sita. Then the 'deepa' are lit, and their lights can be seen twinkling in the windows to remind people of how the royal couple were guided home.

Several days before Diwali, on a festival called Dussehra, effigies of the demon king Ravana are burnt. On the most important day of Diwali house fronts are lit up, tiny nightlights burn in coloured jars and joss sticks are burnt to perfume the air.

The "deepa" lights also welcome Lakshmi, the goddess of prosperity. She is said to visit homes which are brightly lit and to ensure their good fortune in the coming year. She is supposed to bring the presents which people give at this time: toys, sweetmeats and new clothes. They also send greeting cards, some of them exquisitely painted on leaves or peacock feathers.

Diwali is a festival of rejoicing because goodness has triumphed over evil, light over darkness. Like all New Year festivals, it is a time of looking forward to the future.

Epiphany or Twelfth Night
6th January

Epiphany means "showing forth". On this day Christians remember how Jesus was first shown to three Gentiles (non-Jews) – the Wise Men from the East.

The Wise Men "opened their treasures" and gave the baby presents, gold, frankincense and myrrh. Gold was suitable for a king. Frankincense – a fragrant resin from a tree – was often burnt as a sacred perfume during the worship of God in the Temple. Myrrh was a precious ointment, also with a spicy fragrance, used to anoint dead bodies, as Jesus was one day to be anointed. However, myrrh is also used to rub on the gums of teething babies to soothe them, so you might think it was the most suitable of the three gifts.

Between New Year's Day and 6th January, groups of children in South Germany go from house to house dressed as the three Wise Men. One of them carries a large star on a pole, so they are known as the "star singers". After singing carols they beg for money for some good cause. Before leaving they chalk "C + M +B" and the year, on the door. This means: "Christus Mansionem Benedicat": may Christ bless this house.

On the feast of the Epiphany an old ceremony takes place in the Chapel Royal in St. James's Palace in London. Gifts of money in three purses, symbolizing gold, frankincense and myrrh, are offered to the church on behalf of the Queen. The money is then given to poor people (whose names are put forward by local churches and other bodies).

In Western Europe and America 6th January is the Twelfth Night after Christmas, whereas Russian Christians are starting to celebrate. Their Christmas comes on 6th January and their Epiphany twelve days later. In Italy good children receive more presents at Twelfth Night, this time from a wise but rather ugly white-haired old lady, "La Befana", who travels on a broomstick. For naughty children she leaves pieces of "carbone", sweets which look like lumps of coal.

Like many other holy days, Twelfth Night used to be a pagan festival – part of primitive man's worship of sun, light and warmth in the depth of winter. Burning a Yule log is part of these old beliefs. So is the exciting Festival of Fire, Up-Helly-Aa!, which takes place on Shetland in January, when a Viking ship is burnt.

The Saxons lit bonfires in the fields, and round them farmers would drink health to their farm, their animals and their future crops. This was called "wassailing" – wishing "Waes hal!" (Be whole! or May you flourish!).

Something similar is still done in the village of Carhampton, Somerset, where the cider apple trees are wassailed. Cider is thrown over the trees to ensure a good crop, guns are fired into the branches to frighten away evil spirits, and the villagers chant:

'Old apple tree, old apple tree,
We've come to wassail thee!'

In the Middle Ages Twelfth Night used to be the last day of hearty feasting and boisterous horseplay after Christmas. Today we take down the tree and the decorations and feel rather sad that it is all over.

St. Valentine's Day
14th February

It's great fun to send or receive a Valentine card, but most people have no idea who St. Valentine was, or why unsigned greetings of love are sent on his feast day. It seems likely that he was Valentinus, a priest who was put to death by the Roman Emperor Claudius for being a Christian. The Church probably chose 14th February as his feast day in the hope that it would take the place of the rollicking Roman spring festival of Lupercalia (which the Church disapproved of), when young men and girls celebrated because spring was coming. They danced and feasted, and sometimes drew lots to find a partner.

About mid-February the woods and hedges begin to echo with birdsong again after the silent days of winter, and skylarks are heard singing high above meadowland. So this outburst of birdsong in early spring was also said to be connected with St. Valentine. People imagined that on this feast day for exchanging loving greetings, the birds too chose their mates before nest-building could begin.

An English poet, John Donne, had this in mind when he wrote a poem to celebrate a royal marriage on 14th February, 1613. It began:

> *'Hail, Bishop Valentine, whose day this is,*
> *All the air is thy diocese,*
> *And all the chirping choristers*
> *And other birds are thy parishioners . . .'*

It went on to tell how every year this saint "married" all the birds on his feast day.

25

John Donne was born in the time of Queen Elizabeth I, and in her reign choosing a Valentine of the opposite sex was already popular. The choice was made in a game of drawing lots, and it was the done thing for a gentleman to buy his Valentine a gift – gloves, garters, stockings or even jewellery. This could be quite an expense, and Samuel Pepys, the diarist, often grumbled at what he had to spend on his Valentine. In 1661 he bought a pair of embroidered gloves and six pairs of plain ones for Martha Batten, and he noted in his diary that they cost him forty shillings.

Probably because of the expense involved, the custom of giving costly presents went out of fashion, and in the eighteenth century hand-made cards were given or sent instead. These were decorated with paintings of flowers or hearts enclosing a verse for the loved one. Early Victorians too made their own Valentine cards, decorated in all sorts of ingenious ways, with woven or paper lace, ribbons, tinsel, satin, embroidery, pressed flowers or ferns, feathers, shells, etc. There may be a collection of these in a museum near your home.

After the new Penny Postal Service began, cards and letters could be delivered very cheaply by postmen, without anyone guessing who had sent them. Shops sold ready-made Valentines, brightly coloured, gilded, lace-edged and boxed, and young people might even buy and send more than one, just for the fun of it.

Nowadays greetings can be sent through insertions in the newspaper or Valentine Day telegrams. In 1935 the artist Rex Whistler designed a telegram form for the Post Office and 49,000 copies were sent that year on 14th February. Nowadays about a million cards are sent by post in the United Kingdom every St. Valentine's Day.

The shops are full of glossy cards in early February, and they are fun to look through, but it is much more enjoyable to make your own cards, and they may well be treasured longer by the people receiving them.

Here's a traditional rhyme for St. Valentine's Day:

> *'Good morrow to you, Valentine,*
> *Please to give me a Valentine.*
> *I'll be yourn if ye'll be mine:*
> *Good morrow to you, Valentine.'*

Whichever kind of card you choose, when you send Valentines to sweethearts, or Mums or Dads, or anyone you love, you are remembering St. Valentine whose feast it is, and also taking part in a spring tradition much older than Christianity.

The Birthday of the Prophet Muhammad
End of February

Muslims are followers of the religion called Islam. They believe in one God, Allah. Muhammad is their Prophet. On his birthday Muslims celebrate by feasting and rejoicing together and retelling the story of his life and beliefs. It is a very important day in the Muslim calendar.

Muhammad was born in A.D. 570 in Mecca, and he led an uneventful life until he was about forty. One day when he was praying alone in a cave, he had a vision of an angel who told him to go out and preach that there was only one God, Allah, and that he, Muhammad, was his prophet who was to reform the world. Muhammad believed that he heard the voice of the angel Gabriel speaking to him, and what he heard was written down and collected to make the 114 chapters of the Holy Book, the Qur'an (Koran). It was completed about twenty years after Muhammad's death.

The Koran taught beliefs which were different from those held by Muhammad's fellow-countrymen until that time. The most important difference was that there was only one God, and that he alone should be worshipped.

Some people kept to the older beliefs and continued to worship idols, and there were clashes between them and the followers of Muhammad, but Muhammad was finally victorious, and he declared Mecca the Holy City of the Muslims. This happened in the year 8 A.H. (A.D. 630). The Muslim calendar is counted from the "hijra" or "hejira", Muhammad's journey from Mecca to Medina in A.D. 622.

Every devout Muslim prays five times daily, facing the Holy

City. When possible he worships in a mosque, a Muslim church. A "muezzin" ("summoner") calls people to prayer from the top of a minaret – a tall tower standing at some distance from the mosque. It is every Muslim's duty and hope to make a pilgrimage to Mecca, in the country we now call Saudi Arabia, at least once in his lifetime.

A muezzin calling Muslims to prayer

If you are able to go to the Victoria and Albert Museum in London, you may visit the huge gallery full of Islamic art, beautifully decorated in cool blues, greens, golds and turquoise. It gives you some idea of the careful and intricate way in which Muslims decorate their mosques and minarets.

St. David's Day
1st March

Dewi ("David" in English), was the son of a Welsh chieftain. He was brought up as a Christian and went abroad to learn more about the life of a monk. Then he returned to Wales and founded many monasteries which became centres of religion and learning in the Welsh countryside. The monks lived a simple life of prayer, growing their own herbs and vegetables and offering generous hospitality to anyone in need. Because of David's holiness and his inspiring teaching, he was made a bishop. The centre of his bishopric was in the settlement we now know as St. David's on the western tip of the county of Dyfed.

David is thought to have died on 1st March, A.D. 589, and his shrine at St. David's was a place of pilgrimage in the Middle Ages. Later, when the people of North and South Wales became one nation, he was chosen as the patron saint of Wales.

A legend tells how David suggested that his people should wear a leek in their bonnets during battles so that they could be easily recognized; Welsh Guards are still distinguished by a green and white plume in their black bearskins. At Windsor, on the Sunday nearest St. David's Day, it is now a tradition that every member of the Brigade of Welsh Guards is given a leek by a member of the Royal Family. However, as St. David's Day is celebrated at the beginning of Spring when daffodils (Lent lilies), are blooming, this flower has become a second, more graceful emblem of Wales. David's own emblem is a dove.

It is said that David had a sweet singing voice. He encouraged his monks to sing as well as possible for the glory of God, and perhaps this was the beginning of the Welsh tradition of fine male-voice choirs.

Many churches are dedicated to David in south-west Wales, and if you are travelling there, you might visit the cathedral at St. David's. Other places too are called after the saint, and you may visit Llandewi or Capel Dewi or Ffynon Dewi. ("Llan" is the Welsh word for "church", "capel" is a "chapel", "ffynon" is a well or spring.)

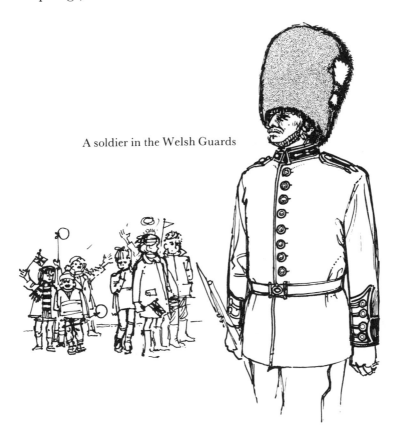

A soldier in the Welsh Guards

St. Patrick's Day
17th March

Although Patrick, or "Paddy", is the most Irish of names, the first Patrick was not Irish by birth. He was born about A.D. 390, probably in west Scotland or Wales, and his family were Christians. At the age of sixteen he was captured by pirates who took him to Ireland and sold him as a slave. He was made to look after pigs and cattle on Mount Slemish in County Antrim in the northeast of Ireland. His solitary life gave him plenty of time to think and pray, and he also learnt to speak the Irish language. After six years he managed to escape and reach the coast. There he found a ship and the kindly captain helped him to return home across the Irish sea to his parents.

Although Patrick was now at home again, he missed the people of Ireland and their country, which he had grown to love, and he wanted to return to tell them about Jesus Christ and his teaching. He went to France, and after studying for some years he was made a priest. He stayed in France until he was nearly forty, and in the year A.D. 432 he returned to Ireland with a few monks.

The pagan king of Ireland, Laoire, generously allowed him to teach and preach throughout the land. Many people became Christians and turned away from the teachings of the Druids, the pagan priests. Patrick built churches and founded monasteries where many people had their first chance of learning to read and write. He was made Bishop of Armagh and grew to be greatly loved by the people of Ireland.

Legends grew up about him. It is said that while he was praying on Croagh Patrick, a mountain in County Mayo in the west of Ireland, he drove all the snakes into the sea. It is true that

Ireland is one of the few places in the world where no snakes live.

Another well-known story tells how Patrick picked a three-leaved weed growing at his feet, a shamrock, as a way of explaining to the people about the Trinity of God the Father, the Son and the Holy Spirit, and this is why the shamrock is always connected with St. Patrick and Ireland. The chorus of a well-known Irish song refers to St. Patrick's love of the plant:

'It shines through the bog, through the brake, through the mireland,
And he called it the dear little Shamrock of Ireland.'

These legends grew up after his death, but there is a prayer, originally written in Old Irish, which is very likely to have been composed by St. Patrick himself. It is often called "St. Patrick's Breastplate", as it calls on God to shield him from all evils. Here is part of it:

'Christ with me,
Christ before me,
Christ behind me,
Christ within me,
Christ beneath me,
Christ above me,
Christ at my right, Christ at my left,
Christ in the fort, Christ in the chariot-seat,
Christ in the ship . . .'

Patrick died on 17th March, A.D. 461, and Irish people all over the world still celebrate St. Patrick's Day. In England it is a tradition that a member of the Royal Family presents the Irish

Guards with bunches of shamrock, the little weed which is now the emblem of Ireland. The Irish airline Aer Lingus flies out hundreds of thousands of sprigs of shamrock all over the world as 17th March approaches. In Ireland the day may be celebrated by parades through the streets to lively Irish "tin whistle" music, or by a "ceilidh" or "ceidhle" (pronounced "kaylee"), a boisterous get-together for gossip, jokes, music and dancing. Everyone will be "a-wearing of the green": wearing a bunch of shamrock in their buttonholes in memory of the slave boy who became Ireland's greatest saint.

Shrove Tuesday or Pancake Day

The Bible tells us that before Jesus Christ began to teach the people he prepared himself by spending forty days praying in the wilderness. We call these forty days Lent, and Lent is the time when Christians prepare for the great celebration of Easter. Some people still give up a favourite food during Lent, but in the Middle Ages everyone had to go without eating meat or lard or eggs for the whole forty days.

Lent begins on a Wednesday, so on the Tuesday everyone made a good start by confessing their sins to a priest and having them shriven or shrove – in other words, forgiven. That is why the day was called Shrove Tuesday. After confession they cooked a meal of pancakes, using up all the eggs and lard in the house.

Everyone knew that the forty days of "fasting" (doing without certain foods) would be hard, so they tried to enjoy the few days before it began (Shrovetide) as much as possible. Italians call these days "carnivale" and the German name is "Karneval" – "carnival" in English. All these words come from a Latin phrase *carnem levare,* meaning "to put meat aside".

In Italy, the Rhineland in Germany, and South Germany (where Shrovetide is called Fasching), there are days of festivities, with parties, fancy dress competitions, eating, drinking and public merrymaking of all sorts. Processions wind their way through town centres, stopping the traffic and causing an uproar, but nobody minds – carnival time comes only once a year!

In France Shrove Tuesday is still called "mardi gras", which means "greasy Tuesday", when all the grease and fat in the house had to be used up. In the south the day is celebrated with carnivals and flower festivals, like the famous one held at Nice, and all over France schoolchildren enjoy making and eating pancakes (they call them "crêpes"). They also make cardboard masks, perhaps funny or scarey ones, to wear in school and on the way home.

Costumes for Mardi Gras

French settlers in the Deep South of the United States of America and the Caribbean took their Mardi Gras customs with them. There is dancing in the streets to jazz music in New Orleans, or to steel band calypso in the Caribbean. Amazing home-made costumes are produced in brilliant colours, decorated with feathers and sparkling sequins and worn in the processions which dance their way through the streets all night long. In Trinidad celebrations begin at 5 a.m. on the Monday and last until midnight on Shrove Tuesday.

In Britain most of us no longer celebrate on Shrove Tuesday

except by making pancakes. In some places, like Olney in Buckinghamshire, the "Pancake Bell" is still rung in the parish church, as it used to be hundreds of years ago, to remind parishioners to come and confess their sins. The bell is mentioned in a verse written in 1684:

> *'But hark, I hear the pancake bell,*
> *And fritters make a gallant smell.'*

It is said that in 1445 a housewife in Olney was busy cooking the family's pancakes when she heard the Pancake Bell – and she still hadn't been shriven! She raced down the village street to church, still in her apron and holding the smoking frying pan in her hand. A pancake race is still held at Olney, and the women who are competing run with a pan containing a pancake, which they must toss at least three times during the race from the market square to the church.

Pupils at Westminster School enjoy the Shrove Tuesday "Pancake Greaze", when the school cook tosses a pancake over a bar sixteen feet above the ground. Whoever manages to grab the largest piece of it in the scrum which follows wins two guineas.

Elsewhere in Britain Shrove Tuesday was once a day for energetic outdoor activities. Bear-baiting and cock-fighting were popular. The master at Sedbergh Grammar School in Cumbria was paid four and a half pence by each of his pupils every Shrove Tuesday to help him buy a fighting cock.

37

In Chester, Derby and many other places there was an annual free-for-all football game up and down the main street. This still takes place in Ashbourne, Derbyshire. The teams are called the Up'ards and the Down'ards, and which team you belong to depends on whereabouts in the town you were born. The goals, two millwheels, are three miles apart! In Sedgefield, County Durham, the goals are less than half a mile apart; one is a stream, the other a pond, and the ball is traditionally the size of a cricket ball.

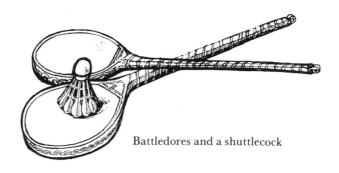

Battledores and a shuttlecock

Another energetic game played in the North and Midlands on Shrove Tuesday was battledore and shuttlecock, rather like today's badminton. In fact, the Leicester name for Pancake Day was "Shuttlecock Day", because so many adults and children played the game in the streets.

At Scarborough in Yorkshire, you not only hear the Pancake Bell on Shrove Tuesday, but also see the townspeople of all ages enjoying the popular custom of skipping along the Foreshore. By long tradition they skip with the strong type of rope used by fishermen. No one quite knows how this custom began, but there is a myth about the Anglo-Saxon god, Tiw (who gave his name to Tuesday), in which he was helped by dwarfs with unbreakable ropes. Perhaps the fisherfolk of Scarborough hoped that by skipping on Tiw's Day, they too would make their fishing ropes unbreakable. Then, when Christians began to observe Shrove Tuesday, the skipping was kept as part of the jollifications before Lent began.

Children used to smash crockery in front of houses, hoping that people would toss pancakes to them. The crashing and smashing was thought to be a noisy way of scaring away the evil spirits of winter and preparing the way for summer. Children used to chant a little begging rhyme as they went from house to house:

> 'Knick a knock upon the block;
> Flour and lard is very dear,
> Please we come a-shroving here;
> Your pan's hot and my pan's cold,
> Hunger makes us shrovers bold:
> Please to give poor shrovers something here.'

Today we can all afford to make pancakes, so I hope that you or someone in your house makes them on Shrove Tuesday. There's a recipe for them at the foot of this page; if you make them yourself, be very careful with the hot fat. If you can't, then try amusing your little brothers or sisters with this action rhyme by Christina Rossetti:

> 'Mix a pancake,   Fry the pancake,
> Stir a pancake,   Toss the pancake,
> Pop it in the pan.   Catch it if you can!'

Pancakes

You need: 100 g plain flour   50 g lard or fat
             a pinch of salt   250 ml milk and water mixed
             1 egg

1 First mix the flour and salt in a basin and crack the egg into it.
2 Stir with a wooden spoon, adding the liquid slowly until all the flour is worked in. Beat the mixture well.

39

3 For each pancake melt a small piece of fat in the pan. When it is really hot, place two tablespoons of the mixture in the pan.
4 When it is golden brown underneath, turn it (or toss it!) and cook the other side.
5 Place the pancake on a warm plate and sprinkle with sugar and lemon juice.

Lent

Ash Wednesday

This is the first day of Lent. All Shrovetide jollity is now over, and in the Middle Ages many people, even royalty, showed their sorrow for their past sins by publicly wearing sackcloth and putting ashes on their heads.

Some Christians still go to church on Ash Wednesday, so that the priest may anoint them on the forehead with a cross of ashes. They are the ashes of palm leaves brought into church on the Palm Sunday of the year before. They were first used for rejoicing and have now been "turned to ashes". As the priest anoints each person's forehead, he says:

*'Remember, man, that thou art dust
And unto dust thou must return.'*

It is a way of expressing sorrow publicly, and also an occasion for thinking about the shortness of life, in preparation for Holy Week at the end of Lent, when Christians remember the suffering and death of Jesus Christ. Statues and crucifixes in Anglican and Catholic churches are covered in purple, for mourning.

The Sundays of Lent

Lent lasts six weeks, which often seemed a very long, rather dull time. Once the first Sunday of Lent was over, people in the North of England counted off the next Sundays on their fingers: "Tid, Mid, Miseray, Carlin, Paum and Paste Egg Day!"

Today no one seems able to explain the first three names – they are probably nicknames taken from Latin psalms sung on those Sundays. "Carlin" is explained on page 43, "Paum" on page 44 and "paste" on page 50.

Mothering Sunday

The fourth Sunday of Lent was the one day in Lent when feasting and games were allowed. Perhaps this is why it was known as "Refreshment Sunday". Today we call it "Mothering Sunday", and it has a long history.

People from outlying hamlets and villages which were too small and poor to keep up a church of their own would journey to the Mother Church of the parish on this Sunday. They would take special gifts and celebrate with the rest of the parish community. So it became known as Mothering Sunday.

In the last two or three centuries it also became the custom for servants, apprentices and other young people who worked away from home to be given the day off on this particular Sunday, in order to visit their parents, perhaps taking a cake or a bunch of flowers for their mothers.

> *'On Mothering Sunday, above all other,*
> *Every child should dine with its mother.'*

The traditional gift of a simnel cake was originally made with "simila", or very fine flour. Today children still like to send a card or bring a gift of flowers to their mother on this day, as a way of saying "thank you" for what she does for them during the rest of the year.

The American name for the day – "Mother's Day" – was officially given in 1906 by the Senate and House of Representatives. They dedicated the day to: "the best mother in the world – your mother".

Carlin Sunday (Passion Sunday)

The fifth Sunday of Lent is still called Carlin Sunday in the north-east of England, although its Christian name is Passion Sunday. It is said that the Scots once laid siege to the city of Newcastle-upon-Tyne, and the inhabitants were almost starving. During the night of the fifth Sunday of Lent, in thick mist a French boat came up the Tyne with a cargo of carlin peas, which saved the lives of the townspeople.

To this day, in the weeks before Easter you can buy these small, greyish peas (delicious served with fried bacon) in the shops on Tyneside and Teesside. They are even served free in some pubs!

Palm Sunday

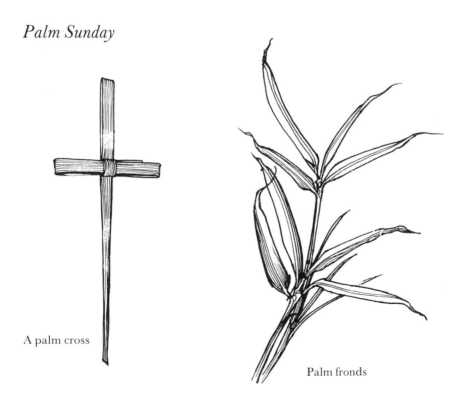

A palm cross

Palm fronds

This was "Paum" Sunday. It reminds Christians of the day on which the crowds waved palm branches to honour Jesus as he rode into Jerusalem on a donkey. On Palm Sunday in the Middle Ages it used to be the custom to go "a-palming" for pussy willow branches to decorate the church and bring good luck to the home. Crosses and fronds of palm leaves are still distributed in Catholic and Anglican churches.

A pussy willow twig

In 1898 a Yorkshireman wrote: "On Paum Sunda' catkins, or lambs' tails, as they are called, are carried in the hand, thrust in the buttonhole, or worn in the hat, whilst many a mantelpiece and ornament is often tastefully decorated with the same."

Holy Week

Maundy Thursday

The last three days before Easter Day remind us of events in the last few days of Christ's life on earth. The church service on Maundy Thursday recalls the Last Supper of Jesus with his twelve apostles. In the early centuries after Christ's death, monks used to wash the feet of poor people on this day, in imitation of Jesus, who washed the feet of his friends before they sat down for their last meal together. Later bishops, princes, popes and kings took part in the foot-washing ceremony on Maundy Thursday.

Edward II, king of England from 1307 to 1327, washed poor people's feet on this day. Edward III gave gifts of food and clothes to the needy. When Queen Elizabeth I was thirty-nine in 1572, she gave to thirty-nine poor women "certain yardes of broad clothe to make a gown and a pair of sleeves". Then she gave them each fish, bread and claret wine, and washed "one foot of every one of the thirty-nine women, in so many silver basins, containing warm water and sweet-scented flowers".

Gradually, the foot-washing ceremony petered out, but monarchs continued giving gifts to the poor every Maundy Thursday. It became the custom for the king or queen to present money, 'Maundy Money', at Westminster Abbey or at some other cathedral, and Queen Elizabeth II continues the tradition. Accompanied by the bishop of the cathedral she walks between two ranks of Yeoman of the Guard, and carries a sweet-smelling nosegay of flowers and herbs – a traditional protection against fever and plague.

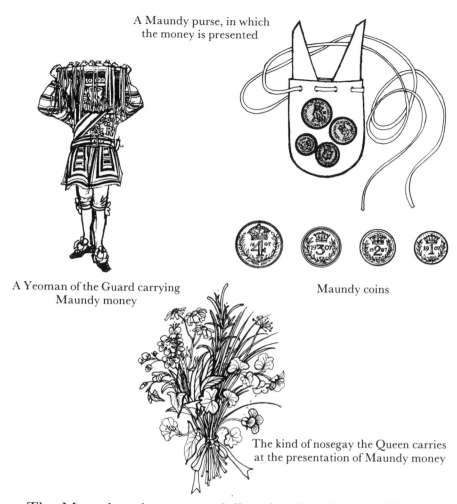

A Maundy purse, in which the money is presented

A Yeoman of the Guard carrying Maundy money

Maundy coins

The kind of nosegay the Queen carries at the presentation of Maundy money

The Maundy coins are specially minted each year. They are not ordinary coins; they are made of silver and are copied from the coins of the time of Charles II. This of course means that they are very valuable. In 1979, when Queen Elizabeth II was fifty-three, they were presented to fifty-three poor people in Winchester Cathedral. The names of the people are suggested by local churches and other bodies, and the ceremony is usually shown on television.

Although the Queen no longer washes poor people's feet on Maundy Thursday, as some of her ancestors did, the ceremony still continues in many Christian churches. Twelve men representing the twelve apostles have their feet symbolically washed by someone representing Jesus. As this is done, a verse from St. John's gospel is sung or read: "I have a new commandment to give you, says the Lord: that you are to love one another as I have loved you." At one time this verse was read in Latin and the Latin word for "commandment" is *mandatum*, which became *mandé* in Old French. When the Normans came to England after 1066, they gradually began to pronounce the word "maundy", as we still do.

Good Friday

This is "God's Friday", on which Christians remember the death of Jesus on a cross outside Jerusalem. In many churches there is a service at or before three o'clock, when it is thought he died. In some countries believing Christians spend the rest of the day quietly. But Seville, a city in the south of Spain, is crowded on Good Friday by thousands of people, all hoping to see the spectacular processions which wind through the streets when darkness falls. By the light of hundreds of flickering candles, richly dressed statues which portray scenes from the last days of Jesus's life are carried aloft.

In Britain, most people, whether Christian or not, like to eat hot cross buns: spicy buns decorated with an egg paste cross, which is a reminder of the cross of Jesus. But the custom of making cakes with crosses is even older. Two were found, still with their crosses on them, in the remains of the Roman town of Herculaneum, which was buried under mud when the volcano Vesuvius erupted in A.D. 79.

The custom – perhaps even the recipe – was brought by the Romans to Britain, and bakers are still producing them by the million every Holy Week. They are delicious halved, spread with butter, sprinkled with brown sugar and heated in the oven until butter and sugar melt together and the outside is crisp.

Perhaps you know the street cry which bakers shouted as they sold their buns.

'Hot cross buns! Hot cross buns!
One a penny, two a penny, hot cross buns!
If you have no daughters, give them to your sons,
One a penny, two a penny, hot cross buns!'

For centuries these buns were thought to have magical powers, and to bring good luck. They were often hung up in a kitchen, or in a farm granary to keep away weevils and vermin, and slipped into a sailor's sea chest to keep him from shipwreck. They were also thought to have healing powers, and after being kept and dried were ground up and mixed with milk or water to make medicine, which was supposed to get rid of various ailments, including whooping cough and stomach upsets.

There are other long-held beliefs about Good Friday. Gardeners, for instance, like to set their main crop of potatoes on this day, partly because it is the right time of year, but also because the Devil has no power over the soil on Good Friday, and therefore there will be a healthy crop.

Easter Sunday

Easter Day is the greatest feast of the Christian year. The preparations of Lent and the sadness of Good Friday are over. In the Bible you can read how, after Jesus died, he was buried in a cave tomb, a sepulchre, and the entrance was blocked by a heavy rock. But when his mother and friends went to the tomb early on the first Easter morning, they found that the huge stone had been rolled away and the tomb was empty. Christians believe that he had risen from the dead and this is called the "Resurrection".

Church services on Easter Day are full of rejoicing: bells ring out, there are colourful flower decorations everywhere, the priest or clergyman wears white vestments to show that it is a glorious feast-day. Congregations used to wear their best clothes (possibly a reminder of times when one's Lenten clothes had to be renewed after being sprinkled with ashes).

In some churches the model of an "Easter garden" is set up. Below a green hill with three crosses, a garden is planted with moss and real flowers. In the side of the hill is a cave, from which a stone has been rolled away to show a tomb, empty but for the linen shroud which wrapped the body.

A cloth called the "Turin Shroud" has recently roused much interest. It is a long cloth with the imprint of a man's body on it. It is claimed to be the very shroud in which the body of Jesus was wrapped after his death nearly two thousand years ago.

Christians think of Jesus as "the Lamb of God"; Christian paintings often show a lamb with a banner and some old inns are still called "The Lamb and Flag". On Easter Saturday Polish children take little baskets of eggs (a pagan symbol) and pieces of sugar-coated lamb (a Christian symbol) to church to be blessed.

Our word "Easter" is said to have come from the name of the Saxon goddess of spring, Eastre. The animal sacred to her was the hare, and perhaps this accounts for the "Easter bunny" often associated with Easter. Somehow he was believed to lay Easter eggs, or at least to hide them in the garden, where children once used to search for them on Easter morning. German children do still hunt out eggs hidden by the "Osterhase" or Easter hare.

Eggs have always been regarded as symbols of new life and re-birth: they seem cold and dead but contain new life, as Jesus came from the tomb at the Resurrection. In ancient times farmers rolled eggs across their fields to encourage a plentiful harvest, and until very recently children always rolled (or "trolled" in Yorkshire) their "pace eggs" or "paste eggs" on Easter Sunday or Monday. ("Pace" and "paste" come from "*Paschalis*", which is Latin for "Easter".) They would go to a nearby park or hillside and roll or troll their hard-boiled paste eggs downhill. Near Preston in Lancashire children still carry on this custom, and on the lawn of the White House in Washington, U.S.A., children and adults in the President's household and many visitors roll their decorated eggs to see which goes the furthest without cracking.

On Dunstable Downs in Bedfordshire local children roll oranges downhill on Good Friday. Some people think this is meant to represent the stone being rolled away from the tomb of Jesus. But, like "trolling paste eggs", it could just as well be the modern equivalent of rolling eggs over the fields to ensure good crops.

Hard-boiled eggs were also used in a game rather like conkers. They were held in the palm of the hand and "jarped" or "jauped" against those of an opponent. The one which cracked first was the loser, and the winner would go on to "jaup" again.

The losers were probably eaten on the spot – eggs were a great treat after six weeks of Lent without any!

During the last days of Lent children must have enjoyed preparing their pace eggs by hard-boiling them in various plant mixtures to dye them. The pasque flower (so called because it flowers at Easter (Paschalis), gives off a brilliant green dye; gorse flowers colour boiling water bright yellow; beetroot makes eggshells rosy red; coffee grounds make them brown; onion skins give a mottled yellow-brown colour; and so on. A little candle wax then rubbed on to the shells gives a bright shine.

In Poland, and the Ukraine in Russia, hard-boiled eggs are beautifully painted with intricate patterns of brilliant colours. Clusters of these jewel-like eggs are arranged in little baskets to decorate the table at Easter.

In Germany the insides of eggs are often blown out, and the empty shells are then carefully painted with colourful designs and hung on threads from leafy branches standing in a pot or vase. These "egg-trees" decorate many homes at Easter, just as fir trees do at Christmas.

The British tradition of colouring eggs is an old one. In the household accounts of King Edward I in 1290 there is an entry of one shilling and sixpence paid out for "four-hundred and a half of eggs" to be covered with gold leaf or coloured to be given away at Easter.

Sometimes drawings were made on the eggs with candle wax before boiling in the dye; then the wax would resist the colouring, and the design or name or date would show up more clearly afterwards. In the Wordsworth Museum at Grasmere in Cumbria you can still see decorated eggs made for the children of the poet William Wordsworth nearly two hundred years ago.

An Easter custom similar to that of going "a-shroving" at the beginning of Lent used to be "pace-egging": going to people's houses in some sort of disguise, hoping for gifts of pace eggs, oranges or perhaps something stronger.

> *'Here's two or three jolly boys*
> *All of one mind,*
> *We've come a pace-egging,*
> *And hope you'll be kind.*
> *We hope you'll be kind*
> *With your eggs and your beer.'*

Like many other traditions which used to brighten the rather dull daily routine of working life, pace-egging has died out. But Easter eggs, made of chocolate and wrapped in shiny paper, are still given as presents on Easter Sunday, and children still enjoy egg-decorating, sometimes for competitions. They produce amazing spiders, space capsules, and cartoon characters which would have bewildered their ancestors. Felt tip pens seem to give the most glowing colours – the old dyeing methods are too slow.

In Biddenden, Kent, a custom which is hundreds of years old continues. A piece of land, said to have been left by the Siamese twins Eliza and Mary Chulkhurst, provides money for a gift of bread and cheese for needy folk at Easter. This is distributed on Easter Monday, and a Biddenden cake is also given out to those who attend the proceedings: a hard biscuit with the imprint on it of two women apparently joined at the side, with only one arm each, as Eliza and Mary Chulkhurst are supposed to have been.

On the afternoon of Easter Sunday the famous Easter Parade can be seen in Battersea Park in London. An Easter Princess rides in a procession which includes hundreds of decorated floats and displays of traditional costumes. A costermonger Pearly King and Queen and members of their family take part, dressed in their amazing clothes which gleam with thousands of mother-of-pearl buttons. There are twenty-five Pearly Royal Families in London, each belonging to a different district.

Easter Monday is a Bank Holiday, and many sporting fixtures and other activities take place over this long weekend.

Passover – Pesach

Around Eastertime Jews celebrate their Passover, a festival that existed long before the first Easter. In fact Jesus himself celebrated the Passover shortly before his crucifixion.

The festival, called in Hebrew Pesach, lasts for a week and there are special services in the Synagogue on the first and last days. However, it is a festival celebrated mainly in the home. On the first night (or the first two) families and friends gather for a Seder: a mixture of a service, history lesson and family party.

During the evening everyone (even the children) will drink four glasses of wine as a sign of rejoicing and everyone will eat from the symbolic foods on the table. These are there to remind the Jews of the time (long ago – about 1250 B.C.) when their ancestors were slaves to Pharaoh, the King of Egypt, and of how Moses, with God's help, rescued them and led them to freedom in their Promised Land. As each of the symbols is displayed or eaten, so another part of the story is told. To start with, the youngest child present asks (in Hebrew) four questions about the Seder, and gradually the answers are given. You will find the questions on page 56.

Parsley is eaten as a reminder of the spring. Before being eaten it is dipped in salt water, a reminder of the tears of the slaves in Egypt, and the Red Sea that parted to allow the Jews to escape. Everyone must eat bitter herbs – horse-radish or onion – to make tears come into their eyes, again a reminder of the tears of the slaves. However, the bitter herbs are dipped into a sweet paste called Charoset (there is a recipe on page 56 for you to make some) that represents the mortar the slaves used to build

54

Pharaoh's cities. The bitter herbs and the sweet paste together remind us that a bitter beginning had a sweet, or happy, ending.

On the table (displayed, not eaten) is a roasted lamb bone. It is a reminder of the lambs the ancient Hebrews killed the night before the Exodus from Egypt. Before cooking the lambs they smeared the blood on the doorpost, and the Bible says this saved them from the plague which affected the Egyptians. All the first-born of the Egyptian families were killed that night, "but the Angel of Death *passed over* the houses of the Hebrews". This is where the name Passover comes from. Of course, Jews today don't kill a lamb or use its blood, they just tell the ancient story.

How the food is arranged on the Passover table

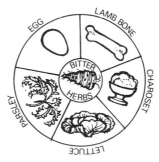

Also on the table is a roasted egg – another reminder of spring.

Finally, there is the matzah or unleavened bread. For the whole week of Pesach Jews eat matzah instead of normal bread. It looks (and tastes) like hard water-biscuits. The Bible says that on the day the Hewbrews left Egypt, there wasn't time to let the dough rise before baking, so the Jews had unleavened bread.

At one point in the Seder the leader hides a special piece of matzah, and children try to find it. If they do they get a special present. Other parts of the Seder are designed to interest the children, and the long evening ends with a collection of children's songs and rhymes. One is rather like *The House that Jack Built* and a new line is added to each verse. Here is the last verse:

Then came the Holy One, blessed be He,
And destroyed the angel of death
That slew the butcher
That killed the ox
That quenched the fire
That burned the stick
That beat the dog
That bit the cat
That ate the kid
Chorus – That my father bought for two zuzim.
Only one kid, only one kid.

The four questions which the youngest child asks are all about why Passover is different from all other nights.

1 On all other nights we eat leavened or unleavened bread; why on this night do we eat unleavened bread only?

2 On all other nights we eat many types of herbs; why on this night do we eat bitter herbs?

3 On all other nights we do not dip herbs even once; why do we dip them twice on this night? (Parsley is dipped in salt water and bitter herbs in charoset.)

4 On all other nights we eat either sitting or leaning; why tonight do we all lean?

The answer to the fourth question is that leaning against the table is a sign of freedom. Can you answer the other three questions from what you have just read about Passover?

Recipe for Charoset

You need: 2 medium apples, peeled and cored; a few dates, stoned; 9 tablespoons seedless raisins; 1 tablespoon candied peel; ½ teacup peeled almonds; cinnamon to taste.

Chop or mince the ingredients very finely, adding cinnamon to taste.

April Fools' Day or All Fools' Day
1st April

Although most people enjoy a practical joke on 1st April, no one seems to know how this custom started. As far back as 1760 *Poor Robin's Almanac* said:

> *'The First of April some do say,*
> *Is set apart for All Fools' Day.*
> *But why the people call it so –*
> *Nor I nor they themselves do know.'*

The most probable explanation is that after the cold, dismal days of winter people were glad to be looking forward to warmer weather and longer days, so they celebrated the beginning of April with a little harmless fooling about, rather like the "mad March hares" they would see racing round the fields. It has been suggested that the first morning in April was the one time in the year when the Court Jester was allowed a rest, so ordinary people had to make up jokes and pranks until he came back on duty at midday.

An even less likely suggestion about the origin of April Fools' Day is to do with Noah, and the time he sent out from the Ark a dove which returned without finding land. Was this the first useless errand or "wild goose chase" in history? Chasing wild geese is probably as difficult as bringing home a bucket of steam, a pint of pigeon's milk or a tin of elbow grease – all well-known Yorkshire errands for children on 1st April.

Some years ago there was a television programme which showed the gathering in of the harvest from Italian spaghetti trees. This fooled millions of people who had forgotten the date.

As far back as 1st April, 1698, a number of Londoners were sent invitations to the 'Annual Ceremony of Washing the White Lions' at the Tower of London – a completely imaginary event.

Scottish children may call one another "April gowk", that is, "April cuckoo" or duffer. In France the favourite insult is *poisson d'avril*, or April fish, and the practical joke is to try to pin paper fish unnoticed on to people's backs. The longer the paper fish stays there, the more enjoyment there is for the spectators, until the moment of discovery when everyone cries *poisson d'avril* at the poor victim – preferably an unsuspecting teacher!

So keep your wits about you on 1st April, and above all, don't go on playing jokes after midday, because then your victim can retort:

'April noonday's past and gone,
You're a fool and I'm none.'

St. George's Day and Shakespeare's Birthday
23rd April

George is said to have been a Christian who became a soldier in the Roman army. The Emperor Diocletian hated Christians, and they went in fear of their lives. Secretly they nicknamed him "Bythios Drakon", which means "Dragon of the Deep", because of his cruelty. When George spoke out against the Emperor's wicked treatment of Christians, Diocletian had him put to death on 23rd April, A.D. 303.

Hundreds of years later Christian soldiers went to the Holy Land to fight in wars called "Crusades", and there they heard stories of George. Some told how he killed a dragon and rescued a princess. These were almost certainly not true (although he *had* resisted Diocletian, the "Dragon of the Deep"), but people liked to think that George was such a brave soldier that he could kill real dragons if necessary.

It was decided to make him patron saint of England, and his battle banner, a red cross on a white background, became the English flag. English soldiers often wore it as a tunic over the breastplates of their armour, so as to be easily identified in battle. Today it is flown in many places on 23rd April, and it still forms part of the Union Flag. After St. George had been declared patron saint of England, his feast day was made a public holiday in 1222, but it is not a holiday nowadays.

In 1348 King Edward III founded the Order of the Garter, which commemorates St. George. It is the highest honour that can be given to a knight, and the oldest in Europe. Every St. George's Day these Knights of the Garter meet in St. George's Chapel, Windsor, wearing their colourful robes, with a medal of

59

St. George and the dragon hanging from a chain round their necks. In 1501 Henry VII and his court celebrated St. George's Day with a knightly joust on the green at the Tower of London.

Brave St. George was a favourite character in "mummers' plays". Mummers or guisers (boys or men, heavily disguised) went from house to house on Christmas Eve, and this custom lasted into the twentieth century in some parts of the country. The mummers would be invited in to act their play and amuse the company, then be offered welcome refreshment.

St. George, dressed in armour, would say:

> *'Here come I, St. George,*
> *That man of courage bold.*
> *If any man's blood run hot,*
> *I'm sure to make it cold.*
> *I slew the fearful dragon, and brought him to the slaughter,*
> *And by that means I won the King of Egypt's daughter . . .'*

The "dragon" might introduce himself like this:

> *'My head is made of iron,*
> *My body is made of steel,*
> *My fingers are made of beaten brass,*
> *No man can make me feel . . . !'*

George was also depicted, killing a fearsome dragon, on the reverse of those old British coins known as "crowns"; and, of course, on the George Cross, a medal given "For Gallantry". You may know a pub called "The George and Dragon".

There are many pictures of St. George – often with a dragon and a beautiful princess – by famous artists, including Bellini, Mantegna, Tintoretto and Dürer. There is also a fine statue of him in Florence in Italy, by a sculptor called Donatello.

Shakespeare's Birthday

By an odd chance, England's greatest writer, William Shakespeare, was born on St. George's Day, 1564, in Stratford-on-Avon, Warwickshire, and also died on the saint's day in 1616. Every 23rd April is now a day of special pageantry in Stratford, as the bells of Holy Trinity Church ring out. Flags from many nations are unfurled, and the Mayor leads a distinguished procession to lay flowers on Shakespeare's grave at Holy Trinity Church.

He was probably proud to celebrate his birthday on the feast of great St. George. In one of his plays he shows how ordinary English people were stirred by their brave patron saint. Just before his soldiers go into battle, their king, Henry V, tells them to shout: "God for Harry, England and Saint George!"

May Day and Labour Day
1st May

When May begins summer is within sight, and people have always rejoiced over the approach of warmth and plenty. On a wall in the ruins of Reading Abbey you can read the words and music of a joyful song composed by a thirteenth-century monk at the approach of summer:

'Sumer is icumin in . . . Lhude sing cuccu!'

The Celtic tribes of Europe celebrated a feast called "Beltane" at this time of year. Beltane is said to come from the name of the god Baal (which means "Lord") and the Celtic word for "fire". All the fires in the village were put out and a special bonfire was lit – probably as a way of worshipping the god of the sun – and from this central fire people re-lit their own house fires. In Scotland a "Beltane Fair" is still held at this time of year in Peebles.

To encourage their crops to grow well in the warmth of the sun, the Celts chose a tree in the centre of their village as a symbol of plentiful growth. It may well have been a hawthorn, commonly known as "may". This tree was decorated with flowers and garlands, and the villagers danced and feasted round it.

The Romans honoured Flora, who was the goddess of flowers, from 28th April to 3rd May, and they too had a tree as a symbol of growth in the centre of their dancing processions. When they invaded Britain they brought their beliefs with them, and their May Floralia festivities became part of British life.

In the Middle Ages and Tudor times, May Day was a great public holiday. Young people got up at dawn to go "a-Maying" in the woods. The girls would wash their faces in the dew, to give them a fair complexion. The song says:

'It's dabbling in the dew makes the milkmaids fair!'

(Milkmaids were famous for their complexions, but the real reason for their lovely skins was that they often caught cowpox from their cows. It was a slight illness which gave them immunity against the much more serious and disfiguring smallpox.) Girls still wash their faces in the dew on May Day at sunrise on the hill named Arthur's Seat in Edinburgh.

Flowers and branches of greenery from the woods were brought to be carried in procession through towns and villages. A Maytime "carol" starts:

> *'We've been a-rambling all this night,*
> *And sometime of this day;*
> *And now returning back again*
> *We bring a branch of May.'*

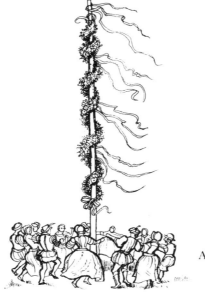

A maypole

63

In the centre of the procession was a "maypole", the trimmed trunk of a hawthorn or "may" tree, decorated with garlands and ribbons. Dancing and other festivities took place around it. A well-known seventeenth century song goes:

> 'Come, lasses and lads, get leave of your dads,
> And away to the maypole hie,
> For every fair has a sweetheart there,
> And the fiddler's standing by . . .'

A May Queen was often chosen from among the village girls. Originally she was supposed to represent Flora, so she sat in royal robes, crowned with flowers, to watch over the merrymaking. Sometimes Morris dances were performed to the music of fiddles and accordions, and sometimes there was a "May Fair", like the one which gave part of London, Mayfair, its name.

In the time of Queen Elizabeth I, Philip Stubbes wrote rather disapprovingly of May Day goings-on. This is how he described a Maypole procession:

"They have twenty or forty yoke of oxen, every ox having a sweet nose-gay of flowers placed on the tip of his horns: and these oxen draw home this maypole, which is covered all over with flowers and herbs, bound about with strings from the top to the bottom, and sometimes painted with variable colours, with two or three hundred men, women and children following it with great devotion . . . then they fall to banquet and feast, to leap and dance about it, as the heathen people did . . ."

In April 1644, during the Civil War, Parliament ordered that all maypoles should be taken down, and no May Day merrymaking was permitted. When a king returned to the throne once more in 1660, some of the old customs were also restored. In 1661 a maypole 134 feet high was erected in the Strand, London, and remained there for fifty years. On May Day, 1667, Samuel Pepys wrote in his diary: "To Westminster, in the way meeting many milkmaids with their garlands upon their pails, dancing with a fiddler before them . . ."

The traditional Morris dancers, eight men wearing hats and clothes of white, criss-crossed with ribbons, and white socks sewn with bells, still perform at many May celebrations. Part of their dancing involves kicking and stamping to make the bells jingle. Sometimes they carry sticks or swords, sometimes white handkerchiefs, and their stamping dance through the village was once thought to wake up the good spirits of the soil so that they would produce a plentiful harvest; their sticks and swords would scare away the evil spirits of winter. Those thirsty Morris men may well have enjoyed a refreshing drink of syllabub, traditional on May Day. It is a mixture of cream and milk, curdled by stirring in wine or cider, then sweetened and beaten up until frothy.

Nowadays the choir boys of Magdalen College, Oxford, are probably among the first to greet May Day, by singing a May morning carol from the top of the chapel tower at six o'clock. There are May Day celebrations at Welford-on-Avon and at Stratford in Warwickshire, at Gawthorne in Yorkshire and at Knutsford in Cheshire.

In Padstow, Cornwall, the hobby-horse appears on 1st May. His body is hidden by a six-foot hoop covered by tarpaulin. He wears a mask and a tall pointed hat. He is accompanied by the "Teaser", who carries a padded club. They dance to music round the town to the traditional song:

'Unite and unite, let us unite
For Summer is a-cuman today.'

From time to time the 'Oss sinks to the ground as though dying (like winter), then suddenly springs to life again (like crops in summer). By mid-afternoon they reach the maypole in the market place and dance round it.

In Minehead, Somerset, 1st May is also called the "Hobby-horse Festival". A ten-foot-long hobby horse, decorated with ribbons, is carried through the streets accompanied by music and dancing.

In Helston, Cornwall, the Furry Dance takes place near the beginning of May. Festivities start when groups of Helston people go into the surrounding countryside to gather bluebells and greenery to decorate their houses and doorways. Later the townspeople gather in front of the market house in their best clothes, then dance through the streets to the music of the famous Furry Dance:

> *'For summer is a-come O*
> *And winter is a-gone O.'*

The name "Furry" perhaps comes from the Cornish word "feur", meaning a fair or celebration.

Another Maytime link with pagan days is the occasional appearance in processions of a figure dressed in green, covered in leaves and branches. At Knutsford he is called "Jack-in-the-Green". Elsewhere he is known as "Jack-in-the-Bush", "Man in the Oak", "The Green Man", and so on. He is said to symbolize growth. He mimes "dying" for winter, then "returns to life" immediately to symbolize summer's new life. A "Green Man" used to walk in London's May Day procession, and there are still pubs

called "The Green Man" and "Jack-in-the-Bush". He also appears as a carved figure in churches, for instance in Holy Trinity Church, Coventry, where a misericord carved under a wooden seat shows a man's face peering from intertwined branches, with two leaves growing from his mouth. In Worcester Cathedral there is a misericord of a man holding flowers or branches.

In France on May Day people give bunches of sweet-smelling lilies-of-the-valley to friends and members of the family.

Labour Day

At the end of the nineteenth century Socialist parties in various European countries gave the name "Labour Day" to 1st May, making it a kind of festival for workers; "labour" is another word for "work". It is a public holiday in some countries. The May Day parade through Moscow or Leningrad is often shown on television news programmes on 1st May; it is mainly a display of the power of the Soviet Union, very different from the carefree rejoicing on village greens in past centuries.

Wesak, the Birthday of the Buddha
May

On the festival of Wesak, at the first full moon in May, Buddhists celebrate the birth of the Buddha, his "enlightenment" and his death.

The Buddha (the word means "the enlightened one") was an Indian prince, Gautama, who was born in the sixth century B.C. He left his luxurious palace to live a life of fasting and meditation. By thirty-five he had found a perfect understanding of the meaning of life and had become "enlightened". For the next forty-five years, until his death, he taught his way of thinking to rich and poor, ignorant and learned.

Buddhist monks

Wesak is rather like Christmas; Buddhists give presents and decorate their houses – with garlands, lighted candles and lamps. They place flowers before statues of the Buddha and release caged birds in memory of the reverence he gave to all living things.

69

Whitsuntide
June

Forty days after Easter Sunday comes Ascension Thursday, when Christians recall how Jesus went up into heaven forty days after he rose from the dead.

At this time of year some villages in Derbyshire decorate their old wells or springs with scenes from the Bible. The pictures are beautifully formed by pressing "anything natural" into damp clay: flower petals, moss, leaves, crushed Derbyshire fluorspar, twigs and berries. Many visitors come to Tissington, Tideswell, and nearby villages to see this old art of "well-dressing".

Ten days later comes Whit Sunday, fifty days after Easter. It corresponds with the Jewish feast of Pentecost, which is celebrated fifty days (hence its name, which means "fiftieth") after Passover. Whit Sunday was once "White Sunday", as many adults were baptised on that day, wearing white robes for the joyful occasion. The first Whit Sunday is sometimes referred to as "the birthday of the Christian Church", since that was the day on which the Holy Spirit came down on Jesus's apostles and gave them the strength to go out and preach.

Whitsuntide was often marked by feasting and fairs, where Morris dancing and performances of "mystery plays" could be watched. These plays were lively re-enactments of scenes from the Bible, and the stage was often an open cart or wagon in the market place. They were called "mystery" plays not because they were mysterious but because they were performed by craftsmen, and a craft was also called a "mystery".

One old Whit Monday custom which has become popular again is the competition for the Dunmow Flitch. In the Essex village of Great Dunmow a mock "trial" is held to find a couple who have never once, "sleeping or waking", regretted their marriage, or wished themselves single again. The prize is a flitch — half a pig, well worth winning.

Whit Walks still take place in Lancashire and Greater Manchester. The walkers are demonstrating their Christian faith and at one time hundreds of people took part, particularly members of the Sunday schools which helped poor children so much in Victorian times.

The Queen's Official Birthday
June

Queen Elizabeth II was born on 21st April, 1926, but she celebrates her "official" birthday publicly on the second Saturday in June.

At 11 o'clock on that morning a Royal Birthday salute is fired in Hyde Park in London. Six 13-pounder guns, dating from 1904, are hauled into position by six horses. The officers and men of the Royal Horse Artillery are in charge, and look resplendent in their full dress uniform of black fur busby, blue jacket with red collar and gold fastenings, blue trousers with a red stripe, jackboots, gleaming spurs and white gloves. They kneel in readiness behind the guns. At precisely 11 a.m. the Royal Salute of forty-one rounds is begun, with a ten-second pause between each round.

The traditional "Trooping the Colour" ceremony also takes place on the Queen's official birthday. This is a ceremony which the Queen always attends, wearing the uniform of the particular regiment whose colours (or regimental flag) is being trooped.

72

In the days when battles took place on open ground with hand-to-hand fighting, it was important that every soldier could immediately recognize the flag of his own regiment, so as to follow it into battle and guard it, if necessary, with his life. So the colour was "trooped", or shown to the troops in a public ceremony. Even today, every year, a different regiment has the honour of trooping its colour publicly and in the Queen's presence on her official birthday. The regiment also gives her a loyal salute.

The Trooping of the Colour takes place on Horse Guards' Parade, a large open space in Whitehall. Massed military bands provide stirring music. The Queen on horseback inspects the troops and then the lines of soldiers in their brightly coloured dress uniforms march to and fro, forming and re-forming to the military music with drilled precision. Now comes the most important part of the proceedings, when the "colour" is paraded for all to see. After this the soldiers march past the Queen in slow and quick time, and the cavalry pass her "at the walk" and "at the trot". You can see most of the ceremony on television. It is a stirring and colourful tradition, which was begun more than two hundred years ago by the Queen's ancestor, King George II.

Midsummer
21st – 24th June

From earliest times people were able to work out that 21st June is the summer solstice – the day in the year when the northern half of the earth is nearest the sun and therefore has most daylight hours. As plenty of sunshine was essential for a good harvest and so for survival in primitive times, bonfires were lit to encourage the sun to shine brightly in the months to come.

The huge slabs and uprights of stone at Stonehenge on Salisbury Plain in Wiltshire were somehow inched into position about four thousand years ago, in the Bronze Age. It is thought that the circle of stones was an immense temple in which to honour the sun god, and perhaps even to offer human sacrifice.

After Christianity had been brought to Britain, the feast of St. John the Baptist was celebrated on 24th June, and this came to be called "Midsummer Day", although mid-summer really falls on 21st June. Throughout Christian Europe people continued to light bonfires and dance round them, but now they were celebrating a Christian feast. They decorated their homes and churches with leafy branches for St. John's Day; these were said to represent the country places in Palestine where John the Baptist preached.

However, some of the old beliefs still lingered on. For example, it was believed that if smoke from St. John's fires blew over the cornfields, the crops would be protected from mildew and other diseases. The ashes from the fires were scattered over the fields to help make the soil richer. In a few places a cartwheel was set alight and rolled, blazing, down a nearby hillside, showing that the sun was now on the turn and its downward journey to winter.

74

There were many beliefs and superstitions concerning Midsummer, often to do with happenings in the future; who was soon to die, and who was soon to marry. There is a bright yellow flower, rather like a little sun, which blooms around 24th June, and is called St. John's Wort. It was considered to have magical properties of driving away the evil spirits and fairy folk who were out working mischief on St. John's Eve. This flower was also used in love charms and to protect houses from fire and lightning. It was best gathered very early on St. John's Eve, while the dew was still wet on it. If a girl slept with it under her pillow that night, she would dream of the man she was to marry. William Shakespeare wrote a play called *A Midsummer Night's Dream*, in which all sorts of tricks are played on human beings by mischievous fairies and a hobgoblin called Puck.

Midsummer was once one of the most popular highdays and holidays of the year, but gradually many of the customs connected with it have died out or been taken over by May Day, which is still celebrated in most countries of Europe.

Independence Day, U.S.A.
4th July

The first English people to settle in America arrived in 1620. Their descendants grew to think of America as their home, whilst still regarding England as their mother-country. The English government thought that the "colonists", as the Americans were known, should still contribute money to England, so they were expected to pay taxes. Gradually they began to resent having to send their hard-earned wealth back to England. They particularly disliked paying duty on imports of tea.

In 1773 some colonists disguised themselves as American Indians and threw about three hundred chests of tea overboard into Boston harbour, as a dramatic gesture of protest. This became known as the "Boston Tea Party". It showed how fiercely the new country wanted the right to govern itself, and not be governed and taxed by the parliament in London. The colonists pointed out that they should not be taxed without having Members of Parliament to represent their opinions; their slogan was: "No taxation without representation".

After much bitterness on both sides, the War of American Independence eventually began in 1775: most of the colonists against England. On 4th July, 1776, the colonists issued a "Declaration of Independence". With this document the history of the "United States" of America began, and 4th July is the date which Americans remember with special pride. The war lasted eight years, but finally the colonists won and were recognized as an independent, self-governing nation.

In the city of Philadelphia hangs the famous Liberty Bell which was rung to celebrate the adoption of the Declaration of

Independence. On it are inscribed the words: "Proclaim liberty throughout the land, unto all the inhabitants thereof." It is still rung every 4th July.

Independence Day is a day when Americans feel particular pride in their community and their country. It is a public holiday and there is no school. Streets and public buildings are hung with flags and decorations; there are historical pageants and military parades, and firework displays or barbecues in the evening. Many people celebrate by a trip to the country or the beach.

In whichever way Americans choose to mark the day, they are all united on 4th July by a feeling of national pride in what they have achieved in the last two centuries. In 1976 there were great celebrations to mark two hundred years of independence.

Bastille Day, France
14th July

If you visit Paris and buy a ticket on the Metro, the underground railway, you may get out at the station called simply "Bastille". A large open square, noisy with traffic, is today the site of what was once the most hated fortress and prison in France: "La Bastille". This grim prison was the symbol of royal tyranny – people were imprisoned there at a word from the king. One of the most famous prisoners was the mysterious "Man in the Iron Mask", an actual person, described in Alexandre Dumas' story of that name.

In the eighteenth century the French peasants were starving and heavily taxed, while the nobility lived in extravagant luxury. A petition to ease the life of the poor was turned down by King Louis XVI, and his wife, Marie Antoinette, when told that they had not even bread to eat, is supposed to have said: "Then let them eat cake."

When the French Revolution began, one of the first targets of the revolutionaries was the dreaded Bastille. A mob of Parisian citizens stormed the fortress on 14th July, 1789, demanding arms and ammunition. The governor of the prison surrendered and handed over his prisoners, who were carried off in triumph. Soon afterwards the Bastille was demolished, and the following year the mob was dancing on its site. You can still just make out the shape of the ancient fortress in the line of the paving stones.

Today the storming of the Bastille is commemorated as a national holiday in France. Celebrations begin the evening before, with processions in most towns and villages. The mayor and other town officials lead the way, followed by the municipal band, the townspeople and perhaps a band of majorettes. The evening may end with a fair, and almost certainly there will be a spectacular firework display going on late into the night. Luckily, as 14th July is a national holiday, most people are able to enjoy a long lie-in the next day!

St. Swithin's Day
15th July

In A.D. 852 a priest named Swithin was made Bishop of Winchester, the most important city in England at that time. When he died ten years later, he was buried, as he had requested, outside his beloved Winchester Cathedral, "under the feet of the passer-by". Later he was regarded as a saint, and when the cathedral was being rebuilt in the reign of William the Conqueror, the cathedral authorities decided that it would be more fitting for St. Swithin's remains to be buried in a splendid new tomb inside the cathedral.

It was arranged that his coffin should be moved to its new position on 15th July, 1077, but when the appointed day arrived, it poured with rain and the ceremony had to be cancelled. It is said to have continued raining for the following forty days and nights, and so people began to wonder whether this was St. Swithin's way of showing his displeasure at having his wishes disobeyed.

The following rhyme from the time of Bishop Swithin's re-burial is still remembered – do you think it ever proves correct?

> *'St. Swithin's Day, if thou dost rain,*
> *For forty days it will remain.*
> *St. Swithin's Day, if thou be fair,*
> *For forty days 'twill rain no more.'*

Ramadan and 'Id-al-Fitr

Ramadan is one of the most important Muslim festivals, the month in which the first revelations of the Koran were made known to Muhammad, the Holy Prophet. The Koran is the sacred book of the Islam religion.

Each time a new moon appears, a new month begins for Muslims. So their year is about ten days shorter than a Christian year, which is based on the movements not of the moon but of the sun. Eventually each Muslim month passes through all the seasons of the year. So Ramadan, although always the ninth month of the Muslim calendar, is observed on slightly different dates each year.

The Muslim calendar is counted from the "hejira", Muhammad's journey from Mecca to Medina in the year Christians call A.D. 622. The European year 1980 was the Muslim year 1400 A.H.

Throughout the whole month of Ramadan faithful Muslims do not eat, drink or smoke from dawn, "when the whiteness of the day becomes distinct from the blackness of the night", until sunset. So they may have breakfast very early in the morning, perhaps at four o'clock, then nothing more until dusk. During the month of Ramadan there are no visits to parties or cinemas, and Muslims try to avoid unkind or dishonest thoughts which might lead away from Allah. They read the Holy Book, the Koran, with particular devotion.

In the hot, dry countries of the Middle East and India, the month of Ramadan means great hardship, as no liquid may be drunk through the hottest part of the day. But each year adults and even children (although the young are not obliged to) faithfully do without food and drink all through the daytime hours for a month.

At the end of the month the preacher, the Imam, announces to the worshippers in the mosque that Ramadan is over, when he officially declares that the rim of the new moon has appeared over the horizon.

Food for 'Id-al-Fitr
a chappatis   *b* jalebis   *c* bean sambal   *d* onion salad   *e* olives   *f* chopped pistachio nuts   *g* poppadoms   *h* Indian samosas (small deep-fried pastries with a spicy potato filling)

This is the signal for a great celebration: 'Id-al-Fitr, the Feast of the Breaking of the Fast. For three days there is feasting; Muslims exchange cards and greetings, and give parties. They try to help people in need at this time, and visit the mosque and the graves of dead members of the family. Muslim children look forward excitedly to the festivities, as special foods are eaten: spicy meat and potato pastries called "samosas", deep-fried "pakoras", carrot pudding and squiggly orange sweetmeats called "jalebi". They also receive presents of money and new clothes in brilliant colours and beautiful materials, richly decorated with embroidery and sequins.

Muslim children look forward to the festivities of 'Id-al-Fitr at the end of the twenty-eight days of Ramadan in much the same way as children in the West look forward to Christmas.

82

Harvest Festivals
July - September

Before Britain became industrialized, most people lived in the country and ate only what they could grow themselves. For them harvest time was the most important in the year, because their food for the winter months depended on it.

By Midsummer the corn was ripening. On 1st August, Lammas Day (from the Old English "hlaf-maesse", the loaf mass), the bread baked from the first corn of the season was brought to church to be blessed. From then on the harvesters were busy from dawn to dusk, reaping the grain and bringing it into the barns.

The very last sheaf in the field was called the Harvest Queen, or the Maiden Sheaf, or the corn dolly. In Devon it was called the "nek", in Wales the "hag", in Yorkshire the "mell doll", and by other names elsewhere. It was decorated with ribbons, flowers and garlands of ivy, and was taken to the farm on the last wagon-load by the singing, cheering harvesters.

> *'We have ploughed, and we have sowed,*
> *We have reaped and we have mowed,*
> *We have brought home every load,*
> *Hip, hip, hip,*
> > *Harvest Home!'*

The Harvest Queen was then put in a place of honour to watch over the Harvest Supper, a huge spread given by the farmer to his men, now that all the crops were safely gathered in. After the supper the Harvest Queen was kept safely until the next "Queen" took her place the following year, and then burned, ploughed into the ground or destroyed in some other ceremonial way. She was never just thrown away, as that would have insulted the corn spirit whom the last sheaf represented. In the village of Altarnum in Cornwall there are some carved bench ends in the village church and you can see a human figure rising from a sheaf of corn – the corn spirit.

During the eighteenth and nineteenth centuries country people developed the craft of making corn dollies in the form of horseshoes, fans and other shapes, and today making corn dollies of this kind has again become a popular hobby.

Nowadays we celebrate the blessings of the harvest by decorating churches with fruits and vegetables, and a service of thanksgiving is held.

But not only the harvests of the fields are celebrated. In Colchester, Essex, the oyster-fishing season opens in September with thanks being given for the harvest of these shellfish. In some places which rely on fishing there is a "Blessing on the Waters" (or boats). At North Shields in County Durham there is an open-air service on the fish quay at which boats and nets are blessed. At Brixham in Devon and Flamborough in Yorkshire, harvest-of-the-sea services are held, and the churches are decorated with nets and fishing gear.

Hallowe'en
31st October

The evening before the feast of All Hallows, or All Saints, on 1st November, is Hallowe'en.

Before Christianity came to Britain the Celts celebrated their New Year's Eve, Samhain, on this night. They believed that spirits, witches and ghosts were about, so they feasted and danced round bonfires which were lit all round the outskirts of villages to frighten away the evil spirits. The ashes of the bonfires were later sprinkled on the fields to ensure a good harvest the following year. (This was intended as a charm, but in fact the ashes probably did help the next harvest in a practical way, since they contained nitrates and other soil-enriching chemicals.)

Nowadays we still have bonfires at this time of year to burn the dead autumn leaves, and we also roast sweet chestnuts and bake apples when they are at their most plentiful, just as the Celts did. But many of the ancient Celtic Samhain activities have now moved five days along the calendar to 5th November, Bonfire Night. Since 1605 this has become a more popular day for traditional autumnal festivities.

However, some of the old games are still enjoyed at Hallowe'en, such as "bobbing for apples". A bowl of water with apples floating on the surface stands on the floor, and the players have their hands tied behind their backs. They must catch the bobbing apples, using only their teeth! On Tyneside Hallowe'en is often known as "Dookie Apple Night."

Another game used to be played by the fire. Girls would try to cut the peel off an apple in one long strip and throw it on the ground to make the initial of the man they would marry.

Until the end of the last century Hallowe'en was often known in parts of Northern England as "Mischief Night". Youngsters would have great fun removing gates from hinges, putting treacle on the door-knockers of unsuspecting neighbours, or running down the street waving a burning besom made of twigs (and previously taken from someone's backyard).

Younger children still enjoy hollowing out swede turnips, cutting holes for eyes, nose and mouth, and putting a candle stump inside. These horrid faces were once thought to scare away evil spirits. After all:

'Hallowe'en, Hallowe'en,
Witches, witches, can be seen.'

Late in October in the Somerset village of Hinton St. George the children hollow out mangel-wurzels to make lanterns. They call them "punkies", and parade through the streets with them on "Punkie Night".

In North America children make even larger "jack-o'-lanterns" by using pumpkins which are later cut up and roasted or made into pumpkin pie. There, Hallowe'en is celebrated with much more gusto and enjoyment than in Britain, since they have no Bonfire Night to follow. The children dress up as ghosts, witches or storybook characters and carry their pumpkin lanterns from house to house. Like many British children on the same night, they knock on the door and demand: "Trick or treat?" Usually they are given a "treat" of money, sweets or candy corn (candy in the shape and colour of a corn cob), or cookies (biscuits), but if they are refused, the "trick" may be a sooty handshake or molasses (treacle) on the door handle or soap smeared on the windows.

Similarly, in the North of England groups of "Hallowe'enies" still go from door to door hopefully chanting:

> *'The sky is blue, the grass is green,*
> *Have you got a penny for Hallowe'en?'*

The State Opening of Parliament
Beginning of November

At the beginning of November members of Parliament re-assemble after the long summer break, or "recess" as it is officially called. On the morning of the Opening of Parliament the 635 Members arrive in good time at the House of Commons. Crowds gather in the streets of Westminster, hoping to catch a glimpse of the Queen arriving in the Irish state coach, escorted by the Household Cavalry in their colourful uniforms.

Meanwhile a forty-one-gun salute has been fired in one of the royal parks, and the cellars of the Houses of Parliament have been searched by Yeomen of the Guard – a tradition which goes back to 1605, when Guy Fawkes and other members of the Gunpowder Plot tried to blow up the King and Parliament.

The Queen is not allowed to enter the House of Commons, since she is not a commoner, so she is met by the Lord Chancellor and led straight to the House of Lords. There, wearing the Imperial Crown, she sits on a magnificent throne at one end of the Upper Chamber, surrounded by nobles, bishops, judges and other important people in their robes and medals. The Queen's messenger, whose title is Black Rod, knocks three times on the door of the Lower Chamber, and at this signal, the Prime Minister, the Leader of the Opposition, and the Speaker of the House of Commons lead the waiting M.P.s along the corridor to the House of Lords. There they stand to hear the Queen's speech.

In fact, the Queen merely reads aloud the speech which has been composed by members of the government. It sets out their plans for the new session of Parliament and lets the public know what sort of laws they hope to make in the following months.

Bonfire Night (Guy Fawkes Night)
5th November

This exciting highday is a fairly new one in the English calendar, but it has taken over some of the older autumn celebrations.

Catholics were unpopular in the seventeenth century, and they feared further persecution. In 1605 a group of Catholic gentlemen asked Guy Fawkes, also a Catholic and a soldier with a good knowledge of explosives, to help them with a horrifying plot. They rented rooms next to the Houses of Parliament and managed to smuggle a ton and a half of gunpowder in barrels into a room directly beneath the House of Lords. At the Opening of Parliament, which always takes place in early November, they hoped to blow up the king and his eldest son, Prince Henry, as well as his ministers, and members of the House of Lords and the House of Commons. Guy Fawkes was to light the fuse.

However, one of the plotters wrote to his brother-in-law and warned him not to attend the Opening of Parliament. The letter was shown to the government and the buildings were searched. Guy Fawkes was taken to the Tower of London and tortured. Eventually, he and seven of the other plotters were found guilty of treason and executed.

The following year the government ruled that since the plot had been discovered and no one had been harmed, 5th November should for ever after be "a day of thanksgiving to be celebrated with bonfires and fireworks". Since then the cellars of the Houses of Parliament have always been searched on the evening before the Opening of Parliament, and 5th November has been celebrated with fireworks and bonfires on which "guys" (effigies of Guy Fawkes) are burnt. Children make the guys themselves and collect money to buy fireworks; they still ask for "a penny for the guy", though a penny doesn't go far nowadays. Letting off fireworks at home can be dangerous and many local authorities now think it safer to put on a public display of fireworks and huge set-pieces. Bonfire Night is also a good excuse for eating traditional goodies: roast chestnuts, baked potatoes, treacle toffee, toffee apples, gingerbread and parkin.

'Remember, remember, the fifth of November,
Gunpowder, treason and plot.
There seems no reason why gunpowder treason
Should ever be forgot.'

Remembrance Day
11th November

November is usually a sombre month, so it seems a fitting time of year to remember the dead, particularly all those who died in World War I (1914–1918) and World War II (1939–1945).

The Armistice, the document which announced the end of fighting in World War I, was signed at 11 a.m. on 11th November, 1918. The time was chosen deliberately – the eleventh hour of the eleventh day of the eleventh month – and until the Second World War, Armistice Day was always remembered on 11th November. After the end of the second war the Sunday nearest to 11th November was chosen as Remembrance Sunday and on that day wreaths of poppies were laid on war memorials and in gardens of remembrance in most towns and villages in the country. The Queen lays a wreath at the foot of the huge national war memorial, called the Cenotaph, in Whitehall in London, and here, as in many other places, two minutes' silence is observed at 11 a.m. In this way the memory of the men and women who died in two world wars is honoured.

The red poppy was chosen for these wreaths and crosses because of a poem written early in the First World War by a Canadian doctor, John McCrae. He was working at a dressing station during violent fighting in the second battle of Ypres. The muddy fields of northern France and Belgium were scattered with dead and wounded men, but flowers still bloomed all round. They inspired Dr. McCrae to write a poem which was published in *Punch* in 1915. It began:

92

'In Flanders' fields the poppies blow
Beneath the crosses, row on row
That mark our place; and in the sky
The larks, still bravely singing, fly
Scarce heard amid the guns below.

We are the Dead. Short days ago
We lived, felt dawn, saw sunset glow,
Loved and were loved, and now we lie
In Flanders' fields . . .'

The blood-red poppy became a symbol of life given in war. If you cross northern France by train or car in summer, you can still see red poppies blowing in Flanders' fields.

After World War I so many servicemen were left crippled or shell-shocked that an organization was founded in 1921 to help them and their families. This was the British Legion, and its members decided to make and sell imitation Flanders poppies every year to raise funds. Nowadays, the "Poppy Appeal" ("Wear your poppy with pride") makes about three million pounds each year.

The Royal British Legion (as it is now called) also organizes an annual "Festival of Remembrance" in the Royal Albert Hall on the evening of Poppy Day in the presence of the Queen. You may have seen it on television. So if you buy a poppy in November, you are not only remembering those who died in past wars, but also your money is helping disabled servicemen and their families living today.

The Lord Mayor's Show
Second Saturday in November

'Hey diddle dinkety, poppety pet,
The merchants of London they wear scarlet;
Silk in the collar and gold in the hem,
So merrily march the merchant men.'

This rhyme may well have been written about the colourful procession which takes place in London on the second Saturday in November. In 1215 King John gave the citizens of London a Charter by which the Mayor was to be elected on 29th September (Michaelmas) and was later to present himself either to the King or to the Royal Justices to be officially installed.

In the early centuries he rode on horseback to the Royal Justices at the Law Courts, or travelled by state barge along the

94

Thames. Today, dressed in his ceremonial robes of scarlet, he rides from Guildhall in the scarlet and gold mayoral coach drawn by six shire horses. This was built in 1757, and is at present kept in the Museum of London at the Barbican, London, where it can be seen in all its shining splendour. It is rolled out for the Lord Mayor's Show every November, then returned to its stand.

Accompanying the coach in the procession marches a guard of honour of musketeers and soldiers with pikes, in their ancient uniforms and helmets. The rest of the procession is made up of servicemen, many bands and numerous floats, decorated to illustrate a particular theme, often connected with the interests or profession of the new Lord Mayor. In 1616 the decorated barges and floats included displays of fish and fishermen, because the new Lord Mayor was of the Fishmongers' Company, and, since his name was Leman, lemon trees often appeared. In 1979 Sir Peter Gadsden was the six hundred and fifty-second Lord Mayor, and because of his interests in mining, the chosen theme was that of our use of natural resources.

WHITTINGTON STONE

SIR
RICHARD WHITTINGTON
THRICE LORD MAYOR
OF LONDON

1397 – RICHARD II
1406 – HENRY IV
1420 – HENRY V
SHERIFF IN 1393

The Whittington Stone on Highgate Hill, on the spot where Dick Whittington and his cat are supposed to have turned back towards London

95

The whole spectacle takes more than thirty minutes to pass by and stretches for a mile through the City of London. Later, the procession returns to the Mansion House, the official residence of the Lord Mayor of London since 1753.

The most famous Mayor was Richard ("Dick") Whittington, who was elected to the office in 1397 and three times more after that. Everyone knows the story of Dick and his cat who were persuaded to tramp back to London to seek their fortunes by hearing the bells pealing: "Turn again, Whittington, Lord Mayor of London". In fact, Richard came from a very wealthy family and never sailed the seas with his cat, but he was most generous to the poor of London, so perhaps making him the likeable hero of a folk tale was their way of showing their gratitude.

Thanksgiving Day, U.S.A.
Fourth Thursday in November

On 6th September, 1620, a group of Dutch and English emigrants sailed from Plymouth in the *Mayflower*. They planned to settle in America, where they hoped to find peace and freedom to live and worship as they wished. It was a sort of pilgrimage, so the seventy-four men and twenty-eight women are remembered as the "Pilgrim Fathers".

After a difficult and dangerous crossing they landed in America, in what is now Cape Cod Bay, Massachusetts, in late December. The pilgrims built log huts and called their first town settlement Plymouth, after the port from which they had sailed. In the spring of 1621 they started to farm the land and sow seed. The native Indians showed them how to grow sweetcorn, sweet potatoes, pumpkins and cranberries, and how to catch and breed wild turkeys. By the autumn of that year the settlers were able to gather in their first harvest. Their leader, the governor of Massachusetts Bay, gratefully invited the friendly Indians to join in a three-day festival of thanksgiving for the blessings of their harvest and of the first year in their new home. We know from their records that their festivities began on a Thursday in November.

Ever since then Americans, particularly in New England, have celebrated this historic harvest festival. Thanksgiving Day and the following day are school holidays, and President Abraham Lincoln officially proclaimed "Thanksgiving" a national holiday in 1863.

Americans celebrate the day with church services and Thanksgiving dinners which are often family reunions. Houses are decorated, particularly with the flowers and fruits of autumn. The

97

Thanksgiving meal includes traditional foods: turkey and cranberry sauce, sweetcorn, sweet potatoes, pumpkin pie and whipped cream. Children enjoy various cookies and candies, including, sometimes, chocolate turkeys! Thanksgiving is also a popular day for watching all kinds of sport, especially football – American style.

St. Andrew's Day
30th November

Andrew was the first of the Galilean fishermen whom Jesus called to follow him. The full story is in the first chapters of the Gospels of Mark and John in the New Testament. After Jesus died Andrew travelled as a missionary as far as Russia and then Greece. There, in the city of Patras, he was taken prisoner and condemned to die for being a Christian. He is said to have chosen to be crucified on a cross "saltire" (which means a cross in the shape of the letter X) because he thought he was unworthy to die in the same way as Jesus. This was probably about A.D. 60–70.

His body was taken to Constantinople. Five hundred years later a group of missionary monks set out from there to tell the Scots about Christianity. They took Andrew's body with them as a protection, and an inspiration in their missionary work. When they landed on the east coast of Scotland they set up an altar and founded a settlement, at the place now called St. Andrews.

Because of his missionary work, his martyrdom and the final resting place of his body, Andrew was chosen as patron saint of Russia, Greece and Scotland. Cypriots, too, celebrate St. Andrew's Day, since he brought the news of Christianity to Cyprus. The Scottish flag is Andrew's diagonal cross in white on a blue background, representing the waters in which he worked as a fisherman. His flag is included in the Union Flag.

St. Andrew's Night celebrations are often held in Scotland, and among Scots living in other countries. These include "piping the haggis" into the dining room; the traditional meat dish of a sheep's heart, liver and oatmeal is carried steaming hot into the room to the music of the bagpipes.

Hanukah, the Festival of Lights
December

Hanukah or the Festival of Lights comes some time in December. The exact date varies from year to year, because the Jewish calendar is different from the English, as we saw on page 19. Hanukah lasts for eight days, or rather eight nights, for all the action takes place in the evening. Every Jewish home that celebrates Hanukah has its own Menorah or Hanukiah – a special eight-branched candlestick. Often every child will have his or her own Menorah.

On the first night of the festival, one candle is placed in the Menorah and, after a blessing is said, this candle is lit, using a special candle called the Shamash or servant-candle whose only task is to light the other candles. On the second night two candles are lit, and so on. On the eighth night all the candles in the Menorah burn brightly.

After the candles are lit the family sing Hanukah songs and then give each other presents. Some families give only one large present on the first night. Others give eight small presents: one on each night.

The children often play with a special spinning top called a Dreidle. It has four sides and on each side is a Hebrew letter. The letters make up a Hebrew phrase which says, "A great miracle happened there". (To play the game the letters are made to mean: take all the money or presents in the kitty; put something into the kitty; take half; or take nothing. Usually children play for sweets.)

"A great miracle happened there" is really what Hanukah is all about. In 165 B.C. Judea was ruled by the Syrian king Antiochus IV. He wanted the Jews to worship idols of Zeus and other Greek gods instead of their own God, and he stopped them worshipping their God in their holy Temple in Jerusalem. Instead he put up an idol there and sacrificed pigs in it to make it unholy for the Jews.

At this a rebellion broke out, led by Judah, the Maccabee, and his brothers. Though heavily outnumbered and without weapons, Judah and his guerrilla army gradually defeated Antiochus and his soldiers. The Jews recaptured Jerusalem and set about cleaning their Temple, ready to re-dedicate it. (The Hebrew word "Hanukah" means "Dedication".) All was ready, but when they looked they could find only one jar of oil with which to light the Temple Menorah. This light was meant to burn continually in the Temple, but one jar of oil would last only one day. However, the Jews had faith and lit the Menorah. The oil lasted for eight days, until new oil could be prepared. This was the miracle that happened there.

Advent
End of November – Christmas

Advent, which means "the coming", starts four Sundays before Christmas, and is the time when Christians begin preparations for the anniversary of the birth of Jesus Christ in a stable in Bethlehem nearly two thousand years ago.

In the early days of the Christian Church the feast day of Christmas was kept on 6th January, but gradually it came to be held on 25th December, at the same time as Roman sun-worshippers were celebrating the birth of the sun. Now Christmas is celebrated all over the world at the same time, but in many different ways. However, Russian Christians still keep Christmas on 6th January.

In Britain the first Sunday of Advent used to be nicknamed "Stir-up Sunday", because one of the prayers said on that day started: "Stir up, O Lord, your power..." Housewives took this as a hint to start preparing the Christmas "plum puddings", which each member of the family helped to stir up – making a wish as they did so.

An Advent garland

German children make an Advent garland of evergreen twigs in which four red candles are fixed. On the first Sunday of Advent one candle is lit, on the second Sunday two candles, and so on. Usually the garland is hung in the hall, perhaps by red ribbons, and reminds the family of the approaching feast day.

Another way of "counting down" to Christmas has also been introduced from the Continent: the Advent calendar. Each day of Advent a little window in the card is opened to reveal a seasonal picture, until on Christmas Eve the final scene shows the stable at Bethlehem.

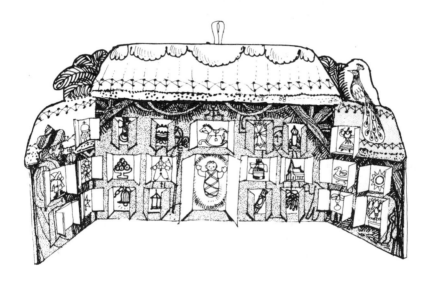

Christmas Eve and Christmas Day
24th and 25th December

At Christmas we remember the birth of Jesus in Bethlehem. There are very many traditions connected with Christmas. This is not surprising when a festival has been celebrated for almost two thousand years and in so many countries. Every nation, even every family, celebrates the feast in a particular way. Some of the most widespread customs are mentioned here, but there are countless other Christmas traditions which you may come across.

On Christmas Eve children in Britain hang a sock or stocking at the end of their bed, in the belief that "Father Christmas" or "Santa Claus" will fill it with toys and good things during the night. When they wake up (very early) on Christmas Day, they are rarely disappointed.

Christmas dinner is usually a family gathering at which the main dish is chicken or turkey with many trimmings, followed by Christmas pudding. An added treat for children is the pulling of crackers at this meal.

The Christmas Tree

For small children one of the most exciting preparations is helping to decorate a fir tree with glittering tinsel, artificial snow, shining bells, balls and lights. The tree will stand in a corner of the home for about two weeks. Prince Albert first made the custom fashionable in Britain when he and his wife, Queen Victoria, were bringing up their own young family; it was a tradition in Germany.

A recent custom is the erecting of a Norwegian Christmas tree in Trafalgar Square, London. Every year since 1946 the people of Norway have sent a huge fir tree to the citizens of London as a way of saying "Thank you" for the kindness they showed to Norwegian troops during World War II. The tree stands in the centre of Trafalgar Square, lit up by six hundred light bulbs.

The Crib

Perhaps you make a crib as part of your home or school preparations for Christmas. On a layer of straw or cardboard you can place crib figures made of folded card, papier mâché, polystyrene, balsa wood, pipe cleaners, plasticine, or almost any imaginable material.

Making a model of the scene in the stable at Bethlehem was the idea of St. Francis of Assisi, who made one for the country people in a forest grotto near Assisi, in Italy, at Christmas A.D. 1223. From Italy the idea spread through the world. Children in Peru place llamas in the stable and Eskimo children place the baby Jesus on a sledge pulled by huskies. French children in Provence make a whole Bethlehem village with farmhouses, a windmill, the mayor, policemen, garlic seller and other unlikely people. In Milan's Cathedral Square in Italy, you can see a huge crib scene in which the figures move by clockwork. In Rome there is now an Exhibition of Cribs every Christmas, which shows handmade cribs from over fifty countries.

Christmas cards

The custom of sending cards at Christmas, like that of decorating fir trees, was introduced in Queen Victoria's reign. The idea may have come from the schoolroom, where children prepared careful messages in copperplate writing, wishing their dear Mama and Papa the compliments of the season.

105

The first printed cards were produced in 1843, and cost one shilling. The central scene was a happy family gathering, while on the left was a picture showing someone charitably "feeding the hungry" and on the right "clothing the naked". Today there are countless designs to choose from, the most popular being holly, robins, snow scenes, Christmas trees, Father Christmas, candles and religious scenes. More than 900 million cards are sold each year, but homemade ones are often the most appreciated.

Food and drink

Christmas has many traditions connected with rich, hot and spicy food, which warms people and drives away thoughts of the cold, dark season outside. This tradition of feasting goes back to the week-long Roman celebration of Saturnalia and the Celtic winter solstice festivities.

In Tudor times the feasts would last eight or nine hours. In those times a boar's head (boar were still hunted wild in Britain) with an orange or apple in its mouth was the centre-piece of the richest Christmas tables. It would probably not be at all to modern taste, although the custom continues at Queen's College, Oxford. Elsewhere peacock, swan and other unusual meats were eaten, as well as the more ordinary goose. After the mid-sixteenth century turkeys became more and more popular. The feast would be washed down with mead or ale. This is described in *Poor Robin's Almanac* of 1695:

> *'Now thrice welcome, Christmas,*
> *Which brings us good cheer,*
> *Minc'd pies and plum porridge,*
> *Good ale and strong beer;*
> *With pig, goose and capon,*
> *The best that can be,*
> *So well doth the weather*
> *And our stomachs agree.'*

Plum porridge was the forerunner of today's Christmas pudding. It was made with raisins, currants, prunes (the "plums"), breadcrumbs and spices, and was eaten with a spoon. Poorer people were more likely to eat frumenty – wheat grains boiled up with milk and sugar. Today's Christmas pudding is supposed to remind us of the gifts of the Wise Men: hidden coins for gold, flaming brandy for frankincense, and the spices for fragrant myrrh.

Mince pies, originally minced mutton pies, were highly seasoned with spices brought for the first time by crusaders returning from the Holy Land. These little pies were oval-shaped to represent mangers, with a piece of pastry lying in the mince, just as Jesus lay in the straw. Eventually they came to be made of spices, fruit and peel.

A wassail bowl

"Wassailers" used to visit every house. Originally they carried a wooden wassail bowl decorated with evergreens and ribbons, full of a kind of hot punch which everyone was invited to share. In Yorkshire the wassail was often known as "Lamb's Wool". The white, frothy pulp from baked apples floated on top of hot, strong ale spiced with cinnamon, cloves and nutmeg.

Carols

Carols are now connected only with Christmas, but originally there were "caroles", songs with accompanying dances, for all the festivals of the year. At Christmas carol singers still go from house to house hoping to be given money, just as the wassailers used to. In some places these singers were known as "Waits".

A very popular carol is this poem by Christina Rossetti, set to music by Gustav Holst; it begins with what we think is a typical Christmas scene.

'In the bleak midwinter
Frosty winds made moan,
Earth stood hard as iron,
Water like a stone,
Snow had fallen, snow on snow,
Snow on snow,
In the bleak midwinter
Long ago.'

When we sing this it is hard to realize that Australians are preparing beach picnics and barbecues for their Christmas dinner.

The most famous carol of all, *Silent Night* (*Stille Nacht* in the original) was written at Christmas, 1818, for the village children of Oberndorf in Austria by the priest, Josef Mohr, and the organist, Franz Gruber. Mice had nibbled through part of the organ bellows in the village church, so the congregation was probably quite unprepared for the sweet sound of the children's voices singing the new carol to a guitar. Now it is sung all over the world on Christmas night.

Evergreens

Before Christmas trees became popular in Britain the traditional form of house decoration was the "mistletoe bough" or "kissing bough". Two metal hoops from barrels were covered with greenery, intertwined ribbons, shining baubles and red apples. A large piece of mistletoe hung in the centre.

Evergreens were already symbols of eternal life in pagan times, and mistletoe was sacred. It was the plant of peace under which enemies would make up their quarrels, so kissing under the mistletoe is a very old custom. Because the plant seems to grow by magic, without roots in soil as other plants do, it was thought to have magical qualities and was sometimes called "heal-all", because of its use in many country remedies, like mistletoe tea.

Romans used evergreens to decorate their houses for the week-long festival of Saturnalia at the end of the year, and in Britain holly and ivy have become the two favourite shrubs for decorating the house at Christmas. In *The Country Child* Alison Uttley tells how a farmhouse used to be made ready for Christmas.

"They decorated every room, from the kitchen where every lustre jug had its sprig in its mouth, every brass candlestick had its chaplet, every copper saucepan and preserving-pan had its wreath of shiny berries and leaves, through the hall, which was a bower of green, to the two parlours which were festooned and hung with holly and boughs of fir and ivy berries ... Holly decked every picture and ornament. Sprays hung over the bacon and twisted round the hams and herb bunches. The clock carried a crown on his head, and every dish-cover had a little sprig."

Boxing Day
26th December

This is the day after Christmas, the "feast of Stephen", when good King Wenceslaus is said to have looked out and seen a poor man gathering wood on a bitterly cold night. The well-known carol goes on to tell how he and his page boy set out to take gifts to the poor peasant.

At one time the alms boxes in church were opened on 26th December. The money collected over the year was shared out among the poor of the parish, and so St. Stephen's Day became known as "Box"-ing Day. In later times this also became the traditional day for presenting gifts of money to people who had been of service during the year – servants, dustmen, postmen, etc. Some people still speak of giving a "Christmas Box" to the milkboy or paper-girl.

Boxing Day often means the start of the pantomime season; and in many country districts a Boxing Day Meet or Hunt is arranged for people who enjoy the sport.

The season of Christmas festivities used to continue until Twelfth Night, 6th January, and this is usually when school holidays end.

A new year has already begun, a new term is about to begin, and the yearly cycle of highdays, holidays and ordinary days starts once again.

111

Other books which tell you more about highdays and holidays

Facts about interesting days in our year:

British Folk Customs by Christina Hole (Hutchinson)
Assemblies by Roland Purton (Blackwell)

Mixtures of facts and fiction, poetry and stories:

The Spring Book ⎫
The Autumn Book ⎬ compiled by James Reeves (Heinemann)
The Christmas Book ⎭

Special days in the year seen through the eyes of a little girl who lived on a Derbyshire farm towards the end of the nineteenth century:

The Country Child by Alison Uttley (Puffin)

Index

113